Poetry by Doing

Poetry by Doing

New Approaches to Reading, Writing, and Appreciating Poetry

Patricia Osborn

National Textbook Company
a division of NTC Publishing Group • Lincolnwood, Illinois USA

Cover illustrations/photos

Top left
RANDALL JARRELL
Artist's rendering* done from a black and white photograph taken by Ted Russell

Middle left
EMILY DICKINSON
Artist's rendering* done from black and white photograph provided by Harvard University Press

Bottom left
ROBERT HAYDEN
Artist's rendering* done from photograph provided by U.S. Information Agency

Top middle
WILLIAM SHAKESPEARE
Detail from oil on wood, from the Art Collection of the Folger Shakespeare Library

Bottom middle
EDNA ST. VINCENT MILLAY
Detail from oil painting on canvas by Charles Ellis, gift of the artist and Mrs. Norma Millay Ellis to the National Portrait Gallery, Smithsonian Institution

Far right
NIKKI GIOVANNI
Artist's rendering* done from photograph taken by Rick Griffiths, Virginia Polytechnic Institute and State University

*Artist's renderings: LINDA SNOW SHUM

Chapter opening illustrations: ETHLYN PANZIRONI

Published by National Textbook Company, a division of NTC Publishing Group.
©1992 by NTC Publishing Group, 4255 West Touhy Avenue,
Lincolnwood (Chicago), Illinois 60646-1975 U.S.A.
Library of Congress Catalog Card Number: 90-63325
Manufactured in the United States of America.

1 2 3 4 5 6 7 8 9 VP 9 8 7 6 5 4 3 2 1

Dedicated to Ray McNeill,
Bowsher High School's first
principal, who put more
trust in reason than in rules,
and to all the Bowsher students
who have proved him right.

Contents

Acknowledgments

Samuel Allen: "A Moment Please" by Samuel Allen (Paul Vesey) from *I Am the Darker Brother*, copyright 1968, The Macmillan Co., copyright © Samuel Allen.

W. H. Auden: "O What Is That Sound?" copyright 1937 and renewed 1965 by W. H. Auden. Reprinted from W. H. AUDEN: COLLECTED POEMS, edited by Edward Mendelsen. Reprinted by permission of Random House, Inc.

The Blade: Portions of a newspaper article written by Fred Nofziger, travel editor, originally published in the April 20, 1989 issue of the Toledo (Ohio) *Blade*, reprinted by permission of the publisher.

Arna Bontemps: "Southern Mansion" reprinted by permission of Harold Ober Associates, Inc. Copyright 1963 by Arna Bontemps.

Frances Cornford: "Childhood" from COLLECTED POEMS by Frances Cornford, published by Random Century Limited.

E. E. Cummings: "nobody loses all the time" reprinted from *IS 5* poems by E. E. Cummings. Edited by George James Firmage, by permission of Liveright Publishing Corporation. Copyright © 1985 by E. E. Cummings Trust. Copyright 1926 by Horace Liveright. Copyright © 1954 by E. E. Cummings. Copyright © 1985 by George James Firmage.

Walter de la Mare: "Autumn" reprinted by permission of the Literary Trustees of Walter de la Mare and the Society of Authors as their representative.

Emily Dickinson: "A narrow fellow in the grass, "I never saw a moor," "It dropped so low," and "Escape" reprinted by permission of the publishers and the Trustees of Amherst College from THE POEMS OF EMILY DICKINSON, Thomas H. Johnson, ed., Cambridge, Mass.: The Belknap Press of Harvard University Press, Copyright 1951, © 1955, 1979, 1983 by the President and Fellows of Harvard College.

T. S. Eliot: "The Naming of Cats" from *Old Possum's Book of Practical Cats*, copyright 1939 by T. S. Eliot and renewed 1967 by Esme Valerie Eliot, reprinted by permission of Harcourt Brace Jovanovich, Inc.

Kenneth Fearing: "A La Carte" reprinted by permission of Russell & Volkening as agents for the author. Copyright © 1940 by Kenneth Fearing, renewed in 1968 by Kenneth Fearing.

Robert Francis: "The Base Stealer," copyright 1948 by Robert Francis. Reprinted from THE ORB WEAVER by permission of Weslayan University Press.

Robert Frost: "The Road Not Taken" from THE POETRY OF ROBERT FROST edited by Edward Connery Lathem. Copyright 1916, © 1969 by Holt, Rinehart and Winston. Copyright 1944 by Robert Frost.

Dana Gioia: "The Next Poem" copyright 1985, reprinted by permission of the author.

Nikki Giovanni: "Nikki-Roasa" reprinted from *The New Black Poetry*, copyright 1969, by permission of International Publishers Co., Inc.

Robert Hayden: "Those Winter Sundays" is reprinted from ANGLE OF ASCENT, *New and Selected Poems* by Robert Hayden, by permission of Liveright Publishing Corporation. Copyright © 1975, 1972, 1970, 1966 by Robert Hayden.

Samuel Hoffenstein: "A Father's Heart Is Touched" is reprinted from POEMS IN PRAISE OF PRACTICALLY NOTHING by Samuel Hoffenstein, by permission of Liveright Publishing Corporation. Copyright 1928 by Samuel Hoffenstein. Copyright renewed 1955 by David Hoffenstein.

A. E. Housman: "Smooth Between Sea and Land" and "Farewell to Barn and Stack and Tree" from THE COLLECTED POEMS OF A. E. HOUSMAN. Copyright 1936 by Barclays Bank Ltd. © 1964 by Robert E. Symons, 1924, © 1965 by Holt, Rinehart and Winston, Inc. Reprinted by permission of Henry Holt and Company, Inc.

Clement Hoyt: "In That Empty" from *Storm of Stars,* published by The Green World, Baton Roughe, LA, copyright 1976 by Violet Hoyt; by permission for Ester Jean Hoyt, Isabel H. Browning and Vera G. Heath.

Randall Jarrell: "A Sick Child" from THE COMPLETE POEMS by Randall Jarrell. Copyright © 1949 and renewal copyright © 1976 by Mrs. Randall Jarrell. Reprinted by permission of Farrar, Straus and Giroux, Inc.

Elizabeth Knies: "Green" from *From the Window* published by Teal Press, PO Box 4098, Sante Fe, NM 87502, Copyright 1985.

D. H. Lawrence: "Intimates" from THE COMPLETE POEMS OF D. H. LAWRENCE, collected and edited by Vivian de Sola Pinto and F. Warren Roberts. Copyright © 1964, 1971 by Angelo Ravagli and C. M. Weekley, Executors of the Estate of Frieda Lawrence Ravagli. Reprinted by permission of the publisher, Viking Penguin, a division of Penguin Books USA Inc.

Denise Levertov: "The Secret" from *Poems 1960-1967.* Copyright © 1964 by Denise Levertov. Reprinted by permission of New Directions Publishing Corporation.

Norman MacCaig: "Stars and Planets" from COLLECTED POEMS, reprinted by permission of Chatto & Windus/The Hogarth Press, London.

Phyllis McGinley: "The Adversary" and "Without a Cloak" from TIMES THREE, copyright 1944, © 1959 by Phyllis McGinley. Reprinted by permission of Viking Penguin, a division of Penguin Books USA Inc.

John Masefield: "Cargoes" reprinted by permission of the Society of Authors as the literary representative of the Estate of John Masefield.

Edna St. Vincent Millay: "The Unexplorer" from COLLECTED POEMS, Harper & Row. Copyright 1922, 1950 by Edna St. Vincent Millay. Reprinted by permission of Elizabeth Barnett, Literary Executor.

Sylvia Plath: "Stillborn" from CROSSING THE WATER by Sylvia Plath. Copyright © 1971 by Ted Hughes. Reprinted by permission of Harper & Row, Publishers, Inc.

Ezra Pound: "Meditatio" from PERSONAE. Copyright 1926 by Ezra Pound. Reprinted by permission of New Directions Publishing Corporation.

Kenneth Rexworth: "Lion" from *Selected Poems,* copyright 1956 by Kenneth Rexworth. Reprinted by permission of New Directions Publishing Corporation.

About the artist of the chapter opening illustrations

Ethlyn Panzironi, the artist who created the original abstract watercolor paintings that appear at the beginning of each chapter, is well-recognized in the United States and abroad for oil painting and stained glass artwork. She studied formally at The National Academy of Design, New York City, and received her B.F.A. from Mundelein College. She has exhibited extensively in the United States. Her paintings are in numerous private collections, both in the United States and Italy. Ms. Panzironi is professionally associated with her family's studio, the Botti Studio of Architectural Arts, Inc., in Evanston, Illinois, creators of stained glasswork for churches and buildings.

Introduction

As you begin *Poetry by Doing,* get ready to play an active role. There's much more to poetry than passing your eyes over words.

Among other things, you'll be
- sharpening your powers of observation
- focusing in closely on key details
- experimenting with words and ideas
- drawing comparisons
- posing questions and testing your answers
- making connections
- developing the habits of sound reasoning
- experiencing what poetry is all about by thinking it through for yourself
- writing some poetry yourself

The more you get involved, the more you'll gain. You'll discover poetry is about everything that matters to people...home and distant places, sports and war, loneliness and laughter and love. And, through learning by doing, you'll acquire skills and habits that can help you with everything you read. You will come in contact with the world of ideas and discover a self that's awaiting you in poetry.

Poetry by Doing

Seeing the Picture Within the Word

rue or False: 1. One picture is worth a thousand words. 2. A poem can speak volumes. Like most broad claims, both statements are true in some ways and false in others. True, a picture can show details that would take many words to describe. Yet it's also true that just one word can provide you with even more ideas than a picture does.

Think of the words that you use most often and know the best. Chances are that you haven't looked up any of them in the dictionary. You haven't had to because you know them perfectly well:

kitchen, street, ice, tree, wheel

You can bring any of these words onto the "computer screen" of your mind and not only know exactly what they mean but also picture many details about them and recall your feelings toward them. In fact, these words may call up so many ideas that you'd have a hard time explaining all of them.

Take the word *school*, for example.

Can you picture the outside of the buildings you've attended? The hallways? The lockers? What about the classrooms? What details can you picture? In what ways are all the classrooms alike, yet different? What feelings does the word *school* bring to mind? Being bored? Nervous? Eager to leave? Glad to be with friends? A whole mixture of associations?

Here's how a dictionary defines the word:

> **school** (skül), n. 1. an institution for teaching persons under college age. 2. an institution or academic department for teaching in a particular field. . . .7. any place, situation, etc., that instructs or indoctrinates. . . .

Compared to the word that you know from experience, the dictionary definition of *school* sounds flat, dull, and inadequate. And, of course, it is. So the word that you know, complete with its pictures and feelings, is the one that's really alive, and that's what poetry is based on.

Poets choose words with the idea that people who speak the same language will have pretty much the same pictures, feelings, and associations they have. Poems, like jokes, take advantage of the fact that one word can be crammed with ideas. Because poetry and humor rely on your knowing how much one word can say, both are often hard to grasp for someone just learning the language.

When you become an alert reader of poetry, you will realize that reading requires more than just passing your eyes across lines of type. It takes mental exercise and active thinking, which will pay off in increased understanding, not only of poetry but of everything you read.

The Visual Impact of Words

Mexican poet José Juan Tablada has written a series of short poems that are much like snapshots—each captures a picture of an animal. Before you read these poetic snapshots, try to picture the creatures in your mind. How would you describe a tortoise, a monkey, a toad, or a dragonfly?

What do you "see" when you think of a tortoise? Do you picture . . . a clumsy-looking creature, a kind of turtle, with a thick, greyish-green shell, shaped like a platter or a soldier's helmet? Legs, tail, and head jutting out like crumpled rubber tubes? Beady, bulgy, sleepy eyes?

What about a tortoise in motion? Do you see it dragging itself heavily and slowly along, waving its long neck back and forth like a rod, pulling itself tight into its shell?

Choose three of the following. Jot down words and phrases that describe your mental picture of each animal.

1. peacock	2. toad	3. dragonfly
4. monkey	5. hippo	6. chameleon

As you read the following poems, see how your image of each creature fits into the scene.

Images

Although he never stirs from home
the tortoise, like a load of furniture,
jolts down the path.

*   *   *

The tiny monkey looks at me...
He would like to tell me something
that escapes his mind!

*   *   *

Lumps of mud, the toads
along the shady path
hop...

*   *   *

The dragonfly strives patiently
to fasten its transparent cross
to the bare and trembling bough.

———José Juan Tablada
(Trans. Samuel Beckett)

THINKING IT THROUGH

1. Notice how much you help fill in the pictures. Why doesn't a tortoise ever "stir from home"? How is it like "a load of furniture"?

2. Why does a tortoise look as if it "jolts" when it moves?

3. In what ways does Tablada's poetic snapshot of a monkey fit your mental image? What aspect of a monkey's expression might make it look this way?

4. How does describing toads as "lumps of mud" fit your picture of them? By setting the word *hop* off by itself, what does the poet help you to see?

5. Why does a dragonfly seem to have a "transparent cross"? What qualities of a dragonfly's motion makes the description accurate?

Getting the Right Word

Because José Juan Tablada is Mexican, "Images" were written first in Spanish. An Irish writer, Samuel Beckett, translated them into English.

Translating is not easy. It requires coming as close as possible to the poet's meaning. The translator must try to keep the effect of the original language, while making the poem sound completely natural in its translated version.

Here is Tablada's poem about a peacock in Spanish, followed by two different versions in English. Compare the choices of words in the translations, and decide which you find most effective. You might prefer some choices from one translation and some from the other.

The Peacock
(Pavo Real: The Royal Turkey)

Pavo real, largo fulgor,
por el gallinero demócrata
pasas como una procesión...

——José Juan Tablada

Peacock, drawn out shimmer,
you pass like a procession
through the democratic henyard...

(Trans. Hardie St. Martin)

Peacock, splendor extended,
through the democratic chickencoop
you pass like a procession...

THINKING IT THROUGH

1. What words in the translations are similar in spelling and meaning to words in the original version?

2. In one translation, what lines are in different order from the Spanish original?

3. How do the words *henyard* and *chickencoop* create different images?

4. Which comes closer to fitting your image of a peacock, the phrase "splendor extended" or "drawn out shimmer?" Why do you consider one more effective than the other?

5. According to a Spanish-English dictionary, the word *fulgor* means brilliance, radiance. *Largo* means long, abundant, and generous. Would the English version be equally successful if it began in either of these ways?

> Peacock, long radiance
> *or*
> Peacock, abundant brilliance

Explain the reason for your answer.

Experimenting with Words and Ideas

Here are three more poetic snapshots by three different poets. Notice how each depends on you to add what you know and make the picture complete.

> At twilight
> hippo
>   shedding
>   the river
>
> ——Virginia Brady Young

> In that empty house,
>   with broken windows rattling,
>   a door slams and slams.
>
> ——Clement Hoyt

> Green as the inside of a kiwi fruit
> the chameleon
> startled on the pink stucco wall
> races to a tree and turns
> the color of bark.
>
> ——Elizabeth Knies

You can recognize the written snapshots on pages 4 and 5 as poems just by looking at them. Poetry looks different from prose. Poems often follow a pattern. In fact, unlike other writers, poets not only choose the words but also determine the form in which they'll appear on the page.

José Juan Tablada and the other three poets have chosen forms perfect for poetic snapshots. Choose one of them and use it to turn your own mental images into words. Pick a scene that you keep in your own memory album—it can be anything from a creature to a place, something you've seen at home or school or somewhere you've traveled. Put this image into a poem by following the pattern of one of the poems you've just read. Try to use a noun where the poet has used a noun, for example, and an adjective where there's an adjective.

If your poem works, you might want to try more than one. You'll discover that carefully chosen words can create pictures in the mind that are more vivid than any camera can take.

Comparing Ideas

In the following poem, Ezra Pound takes for granted that dogs, no matter how much they differ in looks, have certain qualities in common.

Like many poems, this one asks you to make a comparison and draw a conclusion based on your own experience. It also assumes that, although details may differ, the facts remain the same. So your conclusion and the poet's ought to agree.

Meditatio

When I carefully consider the curious habits of dogs
I am compelled to conclude
That man is the superior animal.

When I consider the curious habits of man
I confess, my friend, I am puzzled.

——Ezra Pound

FOCUSING IN

Answer the following on a separate sheet of paper.

1. The word *carefully* shows that the speaker
   a. has jumped to a conclusion
   b. spent time and effort in thought
   c. is unsure and afraid
   d. doesn't believe the subject is important

2. The word *curious* calls attention to the fact that dogs' behavior can sometimes be
   a. hard to explain
   b. vicious
   c. intelligent
   d. lazy and sluggish

3. By stating "I am compelled," or forced, the speaker implies that he otherwise might have concluded man is
   a. not an animal
   b. not to be blamed for his behavior
   c. not worth considering
   d. not superior

4. Since *dogs* obviously means dogs in general, the reader should assume *man* to mean
   a. all male creatures
   b. male human beings
   c. humans of both sexes
   d. people with superior educations

5. List three qualities that would help the speaker reach the conclusion that "man is the superior animal."

6. Notice how line 4 parallels line 1. This asks for a further comparison, showing man
   a. is not dog's friend
   b. is not really superior
   c. is not a creature of habit
   d. does not make use of his superior qualities

7. By directly addressing the reader as friend and saying, "I am puzzled," the speaker invites the reader to
   a. consider the matter further
   b. feel superior to the poet
   c. decide dogs are superior
   d. get involved in an argument

8. The title *Meditatio* is a Latin word; the closest English version is
   a. After Careful Thinking
   b. A Joking Matter
   c. An Honest Confession
   d. A Superior Opinion

Choosing Exact Words

Poets and other careful writers want their reader's pictures to be as close as possible to their own. Instead of using a lot of words, they often spend much time choosing the one *exact* word to express their meaning.

For that reason, it's helpful to ask yourself *why* a poet chose one word instead of another, similar one. It's part of the thinking process that goes into making an alert reader. Compare the following:

        street <-> boulevard
        highway <-> road
        path <-> expressway
        avenue <-> lane
        alley <-> turnpike

Which are more likely to be found in the city? The country? Arrange the words according to the size of the thoroughfare to which they refer, from the narrowest to the widest. Which ones carry traffic for the longest distances?

As you picture those in the city, what kinds of neighborhoods do they run through? What kinds of buildings do you "see" alongside each?

What different kinds of scenery might those of the country run through?

What is the difference between an avenue and a boulevard? A path and a lane?

Now, in your mind's eye, picture an explorer. Describe the outfit that you see the explorer wearing and the type of exploration to be undertaken. Name three qualities or character traits that you believe an explorer should possess.

Read the poem "The Unexplorer" by Edna St. Vincent Millay. In her poem, Millay has invented or "coined" the word *unexplorer*. Explain how your definition of *explorer* makes her intention clearer.

The Unexplorer

There was a road ran past our house
Too lovely to explore.
I asked my mother once—she said
That if you followed where it led
It brought you to the milk-man's door.   5
(That's why I have not travelled more.)

——Edna St. Vincent Millay

THINKING IT THROUGH

1. What word best describes the mood expressed by the poem—happy, disillusioned, hopeful, regretful, excited?

2. How does the fact that the "road ran past" help you picture the setting of the poem? What do you "see"?

3. What do most explorers look for on their expeditions? How were "the unexplorer's" expectations the opposite of this? Why did the speaker say the road was "too lovely" to explore? What word later in the poem shows the sort of thing "the unexplorer" expected to find?

4. According to the mother's words, "you followed," while "it [the road] led," and the road "brought you. . . ." How are these subjects and verbs different from the ones usually associated with explorers?

5. What proves the last line of the poem is more an excuse than a solid reason for not traveling? How do the parentheses give further support? How can you use line 2 as a better reason for the speaker's becoming an unexplorer?

Filling in the Picture

Poets often use comparisons to provide you with a clearer picture. Comparing one object to another highlights their similarities and makes it easier for the reader to share the poet's image.

Remember, there are more than one kind of comparison.

In Ezra Pound's poem, "*Meditatio*," the poet compares the qualities of dog and man to see which species is superior.

In "The Gray Squirrel," the poet makes two kinds of comparisons. First, he compares how two things look. Be sure to concentrate on the ways that they're alike, not how they are different.

After reading the next poem, try to figure out why the poet chose the comparison and how it helped you picture the squirrel.

This poem also requires you to make a comparison between an animal and a man, in a way similar to "*Meditatio*."

The Gray Squirrel

Like a small gray
coffee-pot
sits the squirrel.
He is not

all he should be,   5
kills by dozens
trees, and eats
his red-brown cousins.

The keeper, on the
other hand   10
,who shot him, is
a Christian, and

loves his enemies,
which shows
the squirrel was not   15
one of those.

——Humbert Wolfe

THINKING IT THROUGH

1. In what way does a gray squirrel look like an old-fashioned coffee-pot? How does the comparison affect your picture of how still the squirrel ''sits''?

2. Assuming that the squirrel does kill dozens of trees, could it do this on purpose? Why or why not? Why would the squirrel eat other squirrels?

3. Should the squirrel know right from wrong, or does it behave according to instincts? When the poet states that ''He is not all he should be,'' should the reader take the poet seriously? Why or why not?

4. What words show that the second half of the poem contrasts the behavior of the gamekeeper with that of the squirrel? Which killings were done purposely? For what reasons?

5. List and compare the verbs used in this poem. All but *shot* and *was* are in what tense? How does this help you picture the moment before the squirrel was shot? How does it help support the poem's criticism of the gamekeeper?

6. Answer question 3 again, substituting "the keeper" in place of "the squirrel." How does this clarify the poem's ending?

7. In what sense is the squirrel a friend of the gamekeeper?

Another Kind of Comparison

Poetry, like other literature, is based on the belief that people share certain qualities, no matter what their place in the world or when and where they lived.

"The Baby" is a poem originally written in Sanskrit, the ancient literary language of India. It was translated by an English poet, Sir William Jones, who lived from 1746 to 1794.

Drop the *st* endings from verbs, and read "you" and "your" in place of "thou," "thee," and "thy" to put the poem into modern English.

The Baby

On parents' knees, a naked, new-born child,
Weeping thou sat'st when all around thee smiled;
So live that, sinking to thy last long sleep,
Thou then mayst smile while all around thee weep.

——Sir William Jones

THINKING IT THROUGH

1. Who is the *you* in this poem?

2. What time of life is described in the first two lines?

3. Why is everyone but the child smiling?

4. What is the grammatical subject of line 3?

5. To what event does the phrase "sinking to thy last long sleep" refer?

6. Another way of saying "So live" would be "Live in such a way." In this case, what does line 4 give as the result of such a life?

7. The poem does not give a direct answer, but what kind of person is the child to become as an adult? Someone who gains much fame, wealth, and power? Or someone who has earned much love, respect, and trust? How does the poem support your answer?

The Fun Side of Poetry

Just as alert readers can share serious feelings, they should also be able to share the not-so-serious ones. Look for the clues and surprise turns that let you know you aren't expected to take the following poem at face value.

A Father's Heart Is Touched

When I think of all you've got
Coming to you, little tot:
The disappointments and diseases,
The rosebud hopes that blow to cheeses,
The pains, the aches, the blows, the kicks,   5
The jobs, the women, and the bricks,
I'm almost glad to see you such
An idiot, they won't hurt you much.

——Samuel Hoffenstein

THINKING IT THROUGH

1. Think about the meaning of the title. Is "touched in the heart" anything like "touched in the head"?

2. How does the first line set the stage for a surprise?

3. Whoever heard of "hopes that blow to cheeses"? Are they like Swiss cheese?

4. By rhyming "bricks" with "kicks," the poet emphasizes the connection among the seven things listed in lines 5 and 6. What is their relationship?

5. Who's an idiot? Who are "they"?

6. Why is it important that lines 1 and 7 have no end punctuation?

7. What proves this dad loves his little idiot? Could you love a father like this? Why or why not?

Sound Carries Sense

So far, you've concentrated on the pictures that words bring to mind. But the sounds of words count, too. Some words are fun to say over and over because of the way they ring in the ear.

It's not always necessary to know the exact definition of a word when sound carries much of its meaning. That's true of words like *scratch*, *crunch*, and *pop*. Soft words, like *soothing*, *fluffy*, and *downy*, often have soft sounds.

And the so-called "dirty" words are mostly short and harsh-sounding. You can spit them out like a verbal firecracker, to startle or snap at someone.

Experimenting with Sounds

Sound is important in choosing a name. Consider the following:

- Smoky, Boots, Snowball, Fluff, Clara, Patches, Muffin

- King, Trevlac, Captain, Brownie, Riggs, Lulu, Scamp.

Which seem more likely names for dogs and which for cats? What is the difference?

List other names that would fit one kind of pet, but not the other.

In "The Naming of Cats," T. S. Eliot shows how much he enjoys the sounds of words and names. Give the poem a first reading, just to discover the unusual names he's invented and the fun he has with words.

The Naming of Cats

The Naming of Cats is a difficult matter,
   It isn't just one of your holiday games;
You may think at first I'm as mad as a hatter
When I tell you, a cat must have THREE DIFFERENT NAMES.
First of all, there's the name that the family use daily,   5
   Such as Peter, Augustus, Alonzo or James,
Such as Victor or Jonathan, George or Bill Bailey—
   All of them sensible everyday names.
There are fancier names if you think they sound sweeter,
   Some for the gentlemen, some for the dames: 10
Such as Plato, Admetus, Electra, Demeter—
   But all of them sensible everyday names.
But I tell you, a cat needs a name that's particular,

(continued on next page)

A name that's peculiar, and more dignified,
Else how can he keep up his tail perpendicular,   15
   Or spread out his whiskers, or cherish his pride?
Of names of this kind, I can give you a quorum,*
   Such as Munkustrap, Quaxo, or Coricopat,
Such as Bombalurina, or else Jellyorum—
   Names that never belong to more than one cat.   20
But above and beyond there's still one name left over,
   And that is the name that you never will guess;
The name that no human research can discover—
   But THE CAT HIMSELF KNOWS, and will never confess.
When you notice a cat in profound meditation,   25
   The reason, I tell you, is always the same:
His mind is engaged in a rapt contemplation
   Of the thought, of the thought, of the thought of his name:
   His ineffable effable
   Effanineffable   30
Deep and inscrutable singular Name.

—T.S. Eliot

17.**quorum**: minimum number.

THINKING IT THROUGH

1. Line 8 comes after Eliot gives Augustus, Alonzo, and Jonathan as examples. Is he serious? How do you know? How do the first four lines offer further proof?

2. Why do lines 11 and 12 leave no doubt about whether Eliot is serious?

3. Eliot obviously invented the names in lines 18 and 19 to represent the second kind of name a cat needs. What words describe this kind of name? According to the poem, what common (or uncommon) quality makes a cat need this kind of name?

4. What is the third kind of name cats need? Who must give them this name? How do the words *thought*, *contemplation*, and *meditation* give a clue to the quality in cats that makes them seem to need this sort of name?

5. *Ineffable* means "not to be spoken," as you might guess from the type of name it describes. Compare it to the words *active* and *inactive*. Does this make you think *effable* is a real word? What about *effanineffable*?

6. Both *unspeakable* and *ineffable* mean "not to be spoken." A violent crime might be described as *unspeakable* but never as *ineffable*. Based on such use, can you explain the difference between these two adjectives? Judging by the poem, why would a name or a sight be *ineffable*?

Appealing to the Senses

Most people can boast of having five senses—sometimes six. The more of these you can engage at once, the higher your degree of concentration and the deeper your involvement.

How many of the senses do video games engage? Does this involvement increase their attraction? Are the games more fun or less without the accompanying sound?

Reading shouldn't be a passive activity. Try to stretch your powers of concentration and participate as much as possible. Begin to watch for appeals to the senses, which help you become more fully involved.

As an exercise, pick a month of the year that is one of your favorites. Then write one or two features that make it appeal to each of the five senses.

Example:

January brings

- the *sight* of trees and rooftops capped in white after an overnight snowfall

- the *sounds* of whistles and bells, shouts and cheers to welcome a brand new year

- the comforting *taste* of a cup of hot chocolate when you come inside from the cold

You may, of course, use other forms of the words *sight*, *sound*, *touch*, *smell*, and *taste*. Try to be as precise as possible in wording your examples, so others can appreciate your choices.

You may choose to present your feelings about your favorite month as a poem. If so, experiment with placement of the words on the page. Notice how variations in positions can change the effect of the images.

Summing Up

When reading poetry, always be aware that the meanings of words go far beyond their formal definitions.

1. Words bring to mind pictures or images that add vividness and life to your understanding of them.

2. Words carry with them associated ideas and feelings that help determine your response.

3. Words can express their meanings through sound, and poets concern themselves with how words sound both individually and in combinations.

Awareness of the different appeals of words is an essential key to understanding poetry.

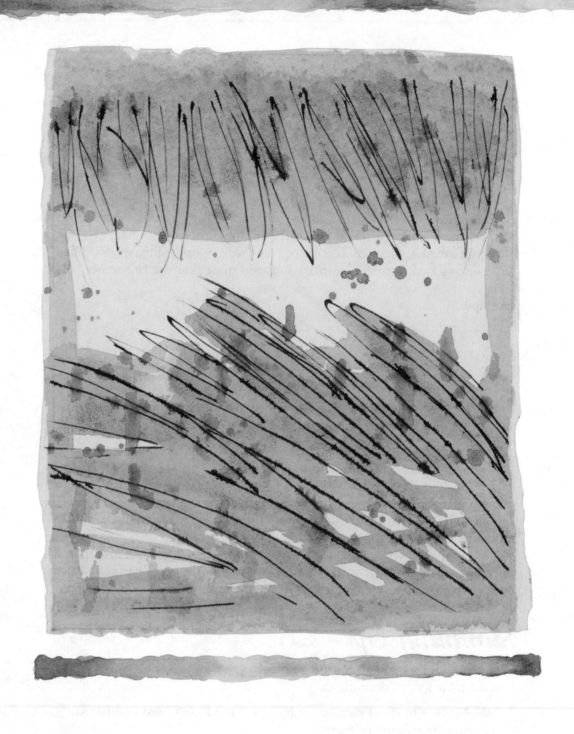

Ballads, Old and New

young or old, it seems part of human nature to enjoy a good story. Today, stories are all around you—on television and VCRs, in movies, magazines, and books.

All these modern storytellers have the ability to repeat a story exactly. Whether in print or on a screen, they record and retell stories in just the same way, scene by scene, detail by detail, the same every time.

This immense treasure of stories is usually taken for granted. It's hard to realize how wonderful it is.

Old Stories

Like so much about people, the love of stories hasn't changed over the centuries. It's not hard to picture ancient folk gathered around a fire, listening to an exciting story.

But did you picture the story being told as poetry?

When most people couldn't read or write, when there was no television or film, they had to memorize stories and pass them on by word of mouth. This made it hard to retell a story without changing it or leaving something out.

EXPERIMENTING WITH WORDS AND IDEAS

To find out how hard it is to keep facts from changing when a story is passed by word of mouth, circulate a joke of thirty to fifty words among six or more people. Have the last person compare the final version with the first one, and see how words and details have changed.

Using Rhyme and Rhythm

What will make a story easier to remember? Add rhyme and rhythm, and it's not half so hard.

Choose a word to rhyme with each of the italicized words that follow, and see how easily you can complete the sense of each line.

1. Inside the *box* was a _____.

2. And with his brother *Frank* he robbed the Chicago _____.

3. He wrote a letter which was large and *long*. . .
   And he promised to do him no _____.

4. If I was to leave my husband dear
      And my two babes *also*,
   O what have you to take me to,
      If with you I should _____?

Rhyme, or the use of words that have the same or similar end sounds, is not just a literary device. It has a very practical purpose—to make a story easier to remember.

Rhythm, the use of a musical beat, sets up a regular tempo that also helps the storyteller remember what comes next. Before the invention of the printing press, rhyme and rhythm were both put to good use as memory devices for storytellers of the oral tradition.

Action + Romance + Courage = Ballad

Ballads are poems that tell stories. They are often set to music and sung. They use rhythm and rhyme. The earliest ballads were the favorite stories of ordinary folk, people who couldn't read or write. For this reason, the tales had to be passed from person to person by word of mouth. Even with rhyme and rhythm, words often changed in retelling. As a result, different versions of the same ballad exist. The "authors" of the original stories have all been forgotten, leaving them anonymous, unknown.

This type of ballad, popular with ordinary people, is called a **folk ballad** and is easy to identify because of its anonymous author.

In some ways all stories and poems are like mysteries. The reader must ask questions and look for clues. Many of the questions will not be answered until the end. If they were answered sooner, it would spoil the fun.

People loved to hear a ballad over and over—just as people today buy a favorite VCR tape and play it again and again. As you reread a ballad, you'll find details and ideas you may have missed the first time. With a bit of practice, you'll become more expert at spotting clues and predicting how they fit together as the plot unfolds.

Ask yourself these questions: Who is the ballad about? What information is revealed about this person? Does this person seem basically good or evil? Where does the story take place? What questions are being planted to arouse my curiosity? What action can I picture in my mind's eye?

"Johnie Armstrong" is a ballad about a Scottish folk hero. As you read, decide what qualities of Johnie Armstrong made ordinary folk look up to him. Were these qualities superficial, such as wealth, popularity, position, and fame? Or were they qualities of character, such as courage, loyalty, pride, generosity, and trustworthiness? Find proof in the poem for the qualities.

As with many folk ballads, some of the rhymes in "Johnie Armstrong" aren't exact because pronunciations have changed over the years. Some words have old-fashioned spellings, too. Sound them as closely as possible to today's English to make the poem easier to understand.

Johnie Armstrong

There dwelt a man in fair Westmorland,
  Johnie Armstrong men did him call,
He had neither lands nor rents coming in,
  Yet he kept eight score men* in his hall.

He had horses and harness for them all.   5
  Their goodly steeds were all milk-white.
O the golden bands around their necks!
  Their weapons, they were all alike.

The news was brought unto the king
  That there was such a one as he   10
That lived like a bold out-law,
  And robbed all the north-countree.

The king he writ a letter then,
  A letter which was large and long,
And signed it with his own hand,   15
  And he promised to do him no wrong.

When this letter came to Johnie,
  His heart was as blythe* as birds on the tree:
"Never was I sent for before any king,
  My father, my grandfather, nor none but me.   20

4. eight score men: 160 followers. **18. blythe**: cheerful or carefree.

(continued on next page)

And if we go to the king before,
  I would we went most orderly;
Let everyman wear his scarlet cloak
  Laced up with silver laces three.

Let everyman wear his velvet coat   25
  Laced with silver lace so white.
O the golden bands all about your necks!
  Black hats, white feathers, all alike.''

By the morrow morning at ten of the clock,
  Towards Edenburough gone was he,   30
And with him all his eight score men,
  Good lord, it was a goodly sight to see!

When Johnie came before the king,
  He fell down on his knee.
''O pardon my sovereign liege,'' he said,   35
  ''O pardon my eight score men and me!''

''Thou shalt have no pardon, thou traitor strong,
  For thy eight score men nor thee;
For tomorrow morning by ten of the clock
  Both thou and them shall hang on the gallow-tree.''   40

But Johnie looked over his left shoulder,
  Good Lord, what a grievous look looked he!
Saying: ''Asking grace of a graceless face—
  Why there is none for you nor me.''

But Johnie had a bright sword by his side,   45
  And it was made of the mettle so free,
That had not the king stept his foot aside,
  He had smitten his head from his fair bodie.

Saying: ''Fight on, my merry men all,
  And see that none of you be taine:*   50
For rather than men shall say we were hanged,
  Let them say how we were slain.''

Then, God wot, fair Edenburough rose,
  And so beset poor Johnie round,
That four score and ten of his best men   55
  Lay gasping all upon the ground.

50. taine: taken.

Then like a mad man Johnie laid about,
  And like a mad man then fought he,
Until a false Scot came Johnie behind
  And ran him through the fair bodie.   60

Saying: "Fight on, my merry men all,
  And see that none of you be taine;
And I will lie down and bleed awhile,
  And then I will rise and fight again."

—Anonymous

THINKING IT THROUGH

1. What mysterious question about Johnie Armstrong is brought out in stanza 1?

2. How does the "news brought unto the king" explain the mystery?

3. Considered alone, does stanza 4 give any hint of the king's real intentions? Support your opinion using words from the stanza itself.

4. Do Johnie's reactions to the letter show him loyal or disloyal to the king? Explain.

5. What does the king's statement "Thou shalt have no pardon, thou traitor strong" (stanza 10) show about his earlier "promise"?

6. In stanza 11, Johnie is looking over his shoulder. To whom must he be speaking, and what makes him look so "grievous"?

7. *Grace* can mean pardon, goodwill, mercy. *Graceless* means lacking grace, elegance, charm; without any sense of rightness. With this in mind, explain Johnie's words: "Asking grace of a graceless face—Why there is none for you nor me" (lines 43–44). What does this say about both their situation and the king's character?

8. What facts in the poem support Johnie's feeling that he and his "merry men" face certain defeat? Explain his attitude toward being "taine."

9. Why does it make Johnie more of a folk hero to have him killed in an attack from behind rather than in a face-to-face fight?

10. The first two lines of stanza 16 (lines 61–62) repeat those of stanza 13 (lines 49–50). Compare the last two lines of these stanzas. How does the last line of stanza 13 help prove that the blow given by the "false Scot" was fatal? Explain why Johnie said his last words and what they show about him.

EXPERIMENTING WITH WORDS AND IDEAS

1. Using words and examples from the poem, decide what inner and outer qualities Johnie had that made him admired by ordinary people.

2. Everyone has an idea of what makes a hero, and those we call heroes often serve as models. Write a description (three to five paragraphs) of someone who fits one of the following categories:
   a. An Extraordinary Hero
   b. An Ordinary Hero
   c. A False Hero

It may be anyone—a famous person, a historical figure, a member of your family, a friend. The only requirement is that you choose someone who represents one of these types of hero.

In your first paragraph, introduce the person and tell why she or he fits your choice. In the body of your paper, include three examples of qualities or actions that make this person deserve your title. Write a concluding paragraph to summarize your proof and convince your reader that your conclusion is correct.

Making the Story Come Alive

One way to bring life to a story is by having characters speak for themselves—in other words, by using dialogue. Folk ballads frequently use this technique.

In "Johnie Armstrong," both Johnie and the king speak. Notice how quotation marks indicate that Johnie's first speech begins with line 19 and continues to the end of stanza 7.

How can you be sure who is speaking? Such words as "he said" often serve as identification, but what if they aren't given?

There are other ways to tell. Line 37 offers one example. The words "thou traitor strong" show that the speaker must be the king, accusing Johnie. Such words of **direct address** often give clues in dialogue.

Quotation marks help, too. It is not the end of a paragraph or stanza but the closing quotation marks at the end of a passage that signal a change of speaker.

Repetition is another technique of the folk ballad. Like rhyme and rhythm, it makes the words easier to remember, but it may have another purpose as well.

In the last stanza of "Johnie Armstrong," a change in a repeated phrase is a signal to make a comparison. Be on the lookout for variations that call attention to important ideas.

The following folk ballad, "Lord Randal," invites you to play detective and figure out the facts of a crime using only the words of two speakers. It's one of the most popular folk ballads because it puts you in the midst of a mystery and asks you to solve the case.

Decide why each question arises logically from the answer before it, and try to draw a conclusion that explains the last stanza and accounts for all of the evidence given.

Lord Randal

"O where hae ye been, Lord Randal, my son?
O where hae ye been, my handsome young man?"
"I hae been to the wild wood; mother, make my bed soon,
For I'm weary wi hunting, and fain wald lie down."

"Where gat ye your dinner, Lord Randal, my son?   5
Where gat ye your dinner, my handsome young man?"
"I din'd wi my true-love; mother, make my bed soon,
For I'm weary wi hunting, and fain wald lie down."

"What gat ye to your dinner, Lord Randal, my son?
What gat ye to your dinner, my handsome young man?"   10
"I gat eels boiled in broo;* mother, make my bed soon,
For I'm weary wi hunting, and fain wald lie down."

"What became of your bloodhounds, Lord Randal, my son?
What became of your bloodhounds, my handsome young man?"
"O they swelld and they died; mother, make my bed soon,   15
For I'm weary wi hunting, and fain wald lie down."

"O I fear ye are poisond, Lord Randal, my son!
O I fear ye are poisond, my handsome young man!"
"O yes! I am poisond; mother, make my bed soon,
For I'm sick at the heart, and fain wald lie down."   20

—Anonymous

11. **eels boiled in broo**: eels boiled in broth.

FOCUSING IN

Answer the following on a separate sheet of paper.

1. Who is the speaker of the first two lines of each stanza?

2. Who speaks in the second two lines?

3. The line in the first four stanzas that does not change is the
   a. first
   b. second
   c. third
   d. fourth.

4. The attitude expressed by the mother's words is
   a. angry and accusing
   b. curious but caring
   c. unfeeling and ignorant
   d. cheerful but rude.

5. Assuming that ''wald'' is another spelling of *would*, the phrase ''fain would'' best fits the meaning of
   a. faintly would
   b. finally would
   c. would like to
   d. would fail to.

6. The mother asks, ''Where did you have dinner?'' and then ''What did you have for dinner?'' By asking questions in this order, the mother shows that she
   a. isn't listening
   b. thinks her son is lying
   c. needs menu suggestions
   d. believes her son is telling the truth.

7. The fact that the mother doesn't question eating ''eels boiled in broo'' indicates she
   a. isn't really paying attention
   b. doesn't consider it odd or unusual
   c. believes he is lying
   d. doesn't like eels.

8. Write the exact words from the poem that describe what happened to the bloodhounds.

9. To make the mystery unfold logically, these words describe the bloodhounds dying of
   a. blood poisoning
   b. gunshot wounds
   c. being run too hard
   d. eating table scraps.

10. Lord Randal says he is "sick at the heart," for he is both literally ill and also heartbroken because
    a. his true-love was not true
    b. his mother nags him
    c. he has been driven to suicide
    d. his plot to murder his girlfriend has backfired.

EXPERIMENTING WITH WORDS AND IDEAS

A different version of this folk ballad, called "Lord Ronald," includes another question about the dinner of eels prepared by the young lord's girlfriend.

"What did she wi' the brew o' them?" the mother asks.

Ronald answers, "She gave it to my hounds for to live upon."

This leaves no question why the bloodhounds "swelld and died."

Write a paragraph explaining which version you like better. Be sure to include reasons for your choice. Ask yourself: Does it add to or detract from the effect of the poem to know for sure that the hounds were fed the broth? Which version fits better with the way other details are handled? Why is "Lord Randal" the more famous version?

Good Guy or Bad?

Even though America was the "new" world, many of the early settlers still couldn't read or write, and they too created folk ballads passed along by word of mouth. As time passed, Americans also created their own folk heroes, basing their legends on actual events. Here's a newspaper article about the real-life outlaw Jesse James, adapted from a recent issue of the (Toledo) *Blade*.

The world's first successful daylight bank robbery was staged in Liberty, Missouri, on Feb. 11, 1866. Today the bank is kept as it was when the James gang rode into town and made off with $60,000.

Compared to 1866, when the average daily wage was 35 to 50 cents, the current purchasing power of $60,000 would be approximately $6.5 million.

Visitors to the bank today hear this story:

"The robbers left the bank, mounted their horses, wheeled them around, and began to leave. One of the robbers shot a youth watching from across the street, a 16-year-old college student.

"A few days later the family received a letter stating that the gang was sorry that the boy was killed, that they had not intended to kill anyone, but just wanted the money. It was signed Jesse James."

After that bank robbery the gang went on for 15 years until Jesse was killed in St. Joseph, Missouri. Loot totaled about $1 million, and some 38 men rode with Jesse (and brother Frank) during those years. Some retired, some were killed, some quit when Jesse was killed, some continued on their own.

Jesse represents the nearest thing we have to Robin Hood. Whether he actually robbed from the rich and gave to the poor, he has that image in folklore, the same as the man who became Robin Hood in England.

Now read the following ballad. Compare the feelings expressed about Jesse James in the newspaper story to those of the ballad. What qualities of Jesse James, Robin Hood, and Johnie Armstrong make them popular as folk heroes?

Jesse James

It was on a Wednesday night, the moon was shining bright,
　They robbed the Danville train.
And the people they did say, for many miles away,
　'Twas the outlaws Frank and Jesse James.

Jesse had a wife to mourn him all her life,　　　　　　　　5
　The children they are brave.
'Twas a dirty little coward that shot Mister Howard,*
　And laid Jesse James in his grave.

---

7. Mister Howard: Thomas Howard, alias used by Jesse James.

Jesse was a man was a friend to the poor,
   He never left a friend in pain. 10
And with his brother Frank he robbed the Chicago bank
   And then held up the Glendale train.

It was Robert Ford, the dirty little coward,
   I wonder how he does feel,
For he ate of Jesse's bread and he slept in Jesse's bed 15
   Then he laid Jesse James in his grave.

It was his brother Frank that robbed the Gallatin bank,
   And carried the money from the town.
It was in this very place that they had a little race,
   For they shot Captain Sheets to the ground.
20

They went to the crossing not very far from there,
   And there they did the same;
And the agent on his knees he delivered up the keys
   To the outlaws Frank and Jesse James.

It was on a Saturday night, Jesse was at home 25
   Talking to his family brave,
When the thief and the coward, little Robert Ford,
   Laid Jesse James in his grave.

How people held their breath when they heard of Jesse's death,
   And wondered how he ever came to die. 30
'Twas one of the gang, dirty Robert Ford,
   That shot Jesse James on the sly.

Jesse went to rest with his hand on his breast;
   He died with a smile on his face.
He was born one day in the county of Clay, 35
   And came from a solitary race.

——Anonymous

T H I N K I N G   I T   T H R O U G H

1. In what ways is "Jesse James" a typical folk ballad?

2. What are the setting and situation at the outset?

3. What attitude is created by the reference to Jesse's wife and children in stanza 2?

4. How could it be possible to shoot a "Mister Howard" and as a result "lay Jesse James in his grave"?

5. What is the purpose of calling Jesse a "friend to the poor" in stanza 3 before mentioning the bank robbery?

6. What attitude does the ballad create toward Robert Ford? Give specific examples and explain the conclusions to be drawn from them.

7. How is the killing of Jesse James similar to that of Johnie Armstrong?

8. How does the poem explain the people's reaction to Jesse James's death? How does the newspaper story further explain it?

9. What does it show about Jesse that he "died with a smile on his face"?

10. How does the expression "came from a solitary race" serve as a fitting epitaph for Jesse, the folk hero?

The Literary Ballad

What were the first items produced serially by machine?

The answer is printed pages.

Thanks to Johannes Gutenberg's invention, printing presses could copy books less expensively, making them available to more people. Printing accelerated the spread of knowledge, making it easier to take advantage of new inventions and ideas, since it was no longer necessary to rely so heavily on memory and word of mouth.

Storytellers and poets, taking advantage of the new technology, invented new forms of literature and found new freedom of expression. Yet people still love stories, as literary ballads prove.

Although modeled after folk ballads, literary ballads were written down and printed. When reading literary ballads, you can assume that the poet has carefully chosen every line, every word, and even every mark of punctuation for a purpose.

Also, it's important to realize that the parts of the story left out of a ballad are often as important as what is given. Being aware of what has been left out and why often enables you to see underlying ideas more clearly.

Farewell to Barn and Stack and Tree

"Farewell to barn and stack and tree,
   Farewell to Severn* shore.
Terence, look your last at me,
   For I come home no more.

"The sun burns on the half-mown hill,   5
   By now the blood is dried;
And Maurice amongst the hay lies still
   And my knife is in his side.

"My mother thinks us long away;
   'Tis time the field were mown.   10
She had two sons at rising day,
   To-night she'll be alone.

"And here's a bloody hand to shake,
   And oh, man, here's good-bye;
We'll sweat no more on scythe and rake,   15
   My bloody hands and I.

"I wish you strength to bring you pride,
   And a love to keep you clean,
And I wish you luck, come Lammastide,*
   At racing on the green.   20

"Long for me the rick* will wait,
   And long will wait the fold,*
And long will stand the empty plate,
   And dinner will be cold."

—A. E. Housman

---

2. **Severn**: river in England. **19. Lammastide**: a harvest festival. **21. rick**: haystack. **22. fold**: pen or flock of sheep.

THINKING IT THROUGH

1. How does the punctuation make clear that there is only one speaker in this poem? Why is the speaker saying good-bye to his farm and to Terence?

2. After reading the poem, how would you identify Terence? Is he most likely the speaker's father, brother, or friend?

3. The full extent of the crime isn't given until lines 11 and 12. Who was the victim, and why will it cause the mother so much grief?

4. The speaker twice refers to the blood on his hands. Does this make him seem bloodthirsty and violent or guilty and regretful? Find other details in the poem to support your conclusion.

5. What three things does the speaker wish for Terence in stanza 5? Does this show the speaker to be basically good or basically evil? Support your answer.

6. How does the last stanza tie together with the first one? What of the speaker's future plans can be inferred from the poem?

Getting Inside the Poem

What's left unsaid in this poem is as important as what is said. The speaker is an ordinary farmer who, like many people, has trouble expressing his innermost thoughts. In order to share his feelings, you have to deduce the depth of his emotions from what he can bring himself to say. Instead of using flowery language, the poet lets the farmer speak naturally of common, everyday things so that the reader senses his difficulty in telling what he feels.

One way to clarify your understanding of such feelings is to write them down as an **interior monologue**. Imagine yourself to be the speaker, adopt his persona, and write the thoughts that might be going through his mind. Here is how you might do it.

> It is hard to believe that I have to leave the place and people I love most forever, all for one minute of blind madness. I must have gone crazy with anger. If there was any way to call back what I've done, I would. But now it's too late. Most of all, I hate what I've done to Mother. She loved both of us, both me and Maurice. Now I have killed him and killed her love for me. After this, she'll think of me as nothing but a murderer. Worst of all, I am leaving her all alone, with no sons left to tend the farm.

What got into me? How could I have done it? Now that I'm leaving, I realize that the little things I took for granted are the most important...the friendship of Terence, the good feel of working up a sweat, Mother's cooking on the table. God, how I'll miss them! What have I done!

Working Together

With another student, determine the speakers in "O What Is That Sound?" Notice there are no quotation marks to guide you. Together, decide what the setting is, what can be concluded about the characters, and how each stanza progresses. Be sure to know what change takes place in the final stanza, and what effect the poem creates at the end.

O What Is That Sound?

O what is that sound which so thrills the ear
  Down in the valley drumming, drumming?
Only the scarlet soldiers, dear,
          The soldiers coming.

O what is that light I see flashing so clear   5
  Over the distance brightly, brightly?
Only the sun on their weapons, dear,
          As they step lightly.

O what are they doing with all that gear;
  What are they doing this morning, this morning?   10
Only their usual maneuvers, dear,
          Or perhaps a warning.

O why have they left the road down there;
  Why are they suddenly wheeling, wheeling?
Perhaps a change in the orders, dear;   15
          Why are you kneeling?

O haven't they stopped for the doctor's care;
  Haven't they reined their horses, their horses?
Why they are none of them wounded, dear,
          None of these forces.   20

(continued on next page)

O is it the parson they want with white hair;
   Is it the parson, is it, is it?
No, they are passing his gateway, dear,
              Without a visit.

O it must be the farmer who lives so near;   25
   It must be the farmer so cunning, so cunning?
They have passed the farm already, dear,
           And now they are running.

O where are you going? Stay with me here!
   Were the vows you swore me deceiving, deceiving?   30
No, I promised to love you, dear,
           But I must be leaving.

O it's broken the lock and splintered the door,
   O it's the gate where they're turning, turning;
Their feet are heavy on the floor   35
   And their eyes are burning.

—W. H. Auden

EXPERIMENTING WITH WORDS AND IDEAS

Choose one of the speakers in the ballad and adopt his or her persona. Then write an interior monologue expressing that person's thoughts as revealed through the dialogue. Some of the ideas may come from your imagination, but be sure the feelings accurately echo the speaker's.

Ballads in Dialect

The following ballad is written in **dialect**. That is, the words are spelled to sound as they do when given a pronunciation peculiar to a certain locality. In this case, the dialect is that of ordinary British soldiers. Note that they tend to drop beginning *h*'s in words like *him* and *hear*. They also drop final sounds, such as *g* and *d*. For easier reading, sound the words to yourself in standard English.

    Speaking are two soldiers, Files-on-Parade and the Color Sergeant, who are known by their military duties. A file is a line of soldiers and colors are the flag. What duty do you think each performs?

Danny Deever

"What are the bugles blowin' for?" said Files-on-Parade.
"To turn you out, to turn you out," the Color Sergeant said.
"What makes you look so white, so white?" said Files-on-Parade.
"I'm dreadin' what I've got to watch," the Color Sergeant said.
    For they're hangin' Danny Deever, you can 'ear the dead march play,   5
    The regiment's in 'ollow square—they're hangin' him today;
    They've taken of his buttons off an' cut his stripes away,
    An' they're hangin' Danny Deever in the mornin'.

"What makes the rear-rank breathe so 'ard?" said Files-on-Parade.
"It's bitter cold, it's bitter cold," the Color Sergeant said.   10
"What makes that front-rank man fall down?" said Files-on-Parade.
"A touch o' sun, a touch o' sun," the Color Sergeant said.
    They are hangin' Danny Deever, they are marchin' of 'im round,
    They 'ave 'alted Danny Deever by 'is coffin on the ground;
    An' 'e'll swing in 'arf a minute for a sneakin', shootin' hound—   15
    O they're hangin' Danny Deever in the mornin'!

" 'Is cot was right-'and cot to mine," said Files-on-Parade.
" 'E's sleepin' out an' far tonight," the Color Sergeant said.
"I've drunk 'is beer a score o' times," said Files-on-Parade.
" 'E's drinkin' bitter beer alone," the Color Sergeant said.   20
    They are hangin' Danny Deever, you must mark 'im to 'is place,
    For 'e shot a comrade sleepin'—you must look 'im in the face;
    Nine 'undred of 'is county* and the regiment's disgrace,
    While they're hangin' Danny Deever in the mornin'.

"What's that so black agin the sun?" said Files-on-Parade.   25
"It's Danny fightin' 'ard for life," the Color Sergeant said.
"What's that that whimpers over'ead?" said Files-on-Parade.
"It's Danny's soul that's passin' now," the Color Sergeant said.
    For they're done with Danny Deever, you can 'ear the quickstep play,
    The regiment's in column, an' they're marchin' us away;   30
    Ho! the young recruits are shakin', and they'll want their beer today,
    After hangin' Danny Deever in the mornin'.

              ——Rudyard Kipling

23. county: men from the same county.

THINKING IT THROUGH

1. What are the setting and the situation in "Danny Deever"?

2. What is going on while Files-on-Parade and the Color Sergeant talk? How do they feel about this?

3. The poem states "the regiment's in 'ollow square." In other words, the soldiers are lined up on four sides of an open space. What is at its center?

4. How does the fact that Danny is considered his "regiment's disgrace" (stanza 3) help explain the purpose for taking his buttons off and cutting his stripes away?

5. The reasons that the Color Sergeant gives for the rear-rank breathing hard and the front-rank man falling down are not logical. Why?

6. Assuming that the real reason has nothing to do with the weather, what did cause the reactions of the rear-rank and the front-rank man? What explains the difference in their responses?

7. What additional information does the second stanza give about Danny's crime?

8. What was the relationship between Files-on-Parade and Danny Deever?

9. What else is told about Danny's crime? Why is this information not given earlier?

10. What is the purpose of bringing the regiment to watch?

11. What is the difference between the first four and last four lines in each stanza?

12. How do Files-on-Parade and the Color Sergeant seem to feel toward Danny?

13. How does their attitude contrast with the one they're "supposed" to have toward him? What words in stanzas 2 and 3 express the "official" attitude?

14. Explain what actually took place in the poem while Files-on-Parade and the Color Sergeant talked.

15. Why are the young recruits especially shaken and why will they "want their beer" so much this day?

EXPERIMENTING WITH WORDS AND IDEAS

"Danny Deever" also provides opportunities for interior monologues. Take the persona of Files-on-Parade, the Color Sergeant, or even one of the raw recruits and see what you discover about their feelings.

Summing Up

Ballads are poems that tell a story and that could be set to music.

Folk ballads were originally passed by word of mouth and have an anonymous author. To make them easier to remember and tell, they used:

1. Rhyme and rhythm

2. Repetition

3. More action than description

4. Dialogue

Literary ballads copy the style of folk ballads but have known authors. Because they are meant to be read, these poems have more freedom of expression.

In Other Words

ike beauty and truth, poetry is easier to recognize and understand than to define. It looks, sounds, and even acts different from other kinds of writing.

That's because, unlike writers of prose, poets control the form in which their words are put on a page. Whether or not it rhymes or has regular rhythm, poetry is usually easy to identify, just by the way it looks.

The Shape of Things to Come

Of course, there's more to poetry than its shape. Consider the following examples. At first glance, each could be termed *poetry* if judged only by form. Yet only one qualifies as a real poem. Try to figure out which one and why.

A

Study proves power of dreams;
Nightmares release daytime stress.

B

Here we are all, by day; by night we are hurled
By dreams, each one into a several world.

——Robert Herrick

C

At night I dream sweet dreams of you,
In daytime you're my dream come true.

——Ann O'Malley

Although all three look as if they could be poetry, only B is a real poem.

Example A has the flat sound of a newspaper headline. It tries to get an idea across quickly so you can decide whether to continue reading or settle for the information already given.

Example C uses both rhyme and rhythm. It can be called verse, but it's not good poetry. It simply pays a pretty compliment, nothing more. In one way, it's like the headline—quick and easy to read.

It's true. Poetry takes longer to read than most prose, except perhaps for scholarly writing. Poems deal with the qualities and questions, the feelings and ideas that make us human. Poetry asks you to stop and think them through.

Poets are constantly inventing different techniques of rhyme and rhythm, new ways of using words and capitalization and punctuation, all to make you pause and ponder and wonder, "Why?"

Notice the rhyming words in example C: *you* and *true*. Those are effortless rhymes like *June* and *moon*, *love* and *dove*. They show that the writer didn't spend much time picking the rhyme, and you needn't waste yours here, either.

But what about *hurled* and *world*? This rhyme invites you to take another look and ask the reason for its choice.

And that's what poetry is about.

Dreams

Here we are all, by day; by night we are hurled
By dreams, each one into a several world.

——Robert Herrick

THINKING IT THROUGH

1. The semicolon divides "Dreams" into two contrasting parts. Since by night each of us is in "a several world," the poem must mean we are all in one world by day. How and why can this be true?

2. *Here* means "at both this time and this place." What image of yourself comes to mind when you read "here we are all"? What meaning in this line would be alike for everyone reading the poem?

3. *Several* means "more than two, fewer than many." How does everyone have "several" worlds when dreaming?

4. The poet could have used the words *different* or *separate* instead of *several* and still maintained the same rhythm. Explain how each would have changed the meaning.

5. What idea does the word *hurled* give about why one enters the world of dreams? How would words like *drifting*, *wafted*, and *carried* change the meaning?

6. With some verbs you can express the same idea in two ways:

   > Casey hurled the ball.
   > The ball was hurled by Casey.

   The second version, called the **passive form**, is generally considered less effective than the first, or **active form**. What are the weaknesses of the passive form of the verb?

7. In this poem Herrick says, "we are hurled/ By dreams," instead of "dreams hurl us." Aside from the need to rhyme, what does his version make clear about the act of dreaming?

8. By beginning the poem, "Here we are all, by day," does the poet emphasize the similarities or differences among people? Which does the second part emphasize? What conclusion does this help you reach?

9. In some ways the poem supports ideas expressed in the headline in example A. How are ideas from the poem similar to those stated in example A?

10. In what ways might having a *several* instead of a *single* world be important to a person when he or she dreams?

Serious versus Humorous Poems

"What do you mean by that?" In a face-to-face conversation, you can ask questions and watch facial expressions and gestures for clues to the meaning of the other person's words. In reading, however, it's just you and the written word.

The careful reader knows this, just as the poet does. Often, difficult words or phrases in poetry are really meant to get your attention, to make you stop and question yourself and the poem, to invite you to engage in a *mental* dialogue—another way of sharing thoughts.

Poetry's advantage as a form of expression is its power to concentrate thoughts. It emphasizes exactness of word choice and meaning. It applies the control of language to put ideas, thoughts, and feelings into perspective.

Those poems that are not ballads or narratives are termed *lyric* poems. This calls attention to the elements of music or song they contain.

As you read the following poem, "Those Winter Sundays," notice how Robert Hayden's precise choices of words and details add a lyric quality to a seemingly ordinary situation.

Those Winter Sundays

Sundays too my father got up early
and put his clothes on in the blueblack cold,
then with cracked hands that ached
from labor in the weekday weather made
the banked* fire blaze. No one ever thanked him.   5

I'd wake and hear the cold splintering, breaking.
When the rooms were warm, he'd call,
and slowly I would rise and dress,
fearing the chronic* angers of that house,

Speaking indifferently* to him,   10
who had driven out the cold
and polished my good shoes as well.
What did I know, what did I know
of love's austere* and lonely offices*?

——Robert Hayden

---

5. banked: made to burn long and slowly. **9. chronic**: constant, continuing for a long time. **10. indifferently**: without interest or concern. **14. austere**: severely simple, harsh, disciplined. **offices**: duties, tasks.

FOCUSING IN

Read the poem through a second time before answering the following questions. Write your answers on a separate sheet of paper. Be sure to find proof in the poem to support your answer.

1. The speaker in the poem takes the viewpoint of a
   a. child being scolded by his dad
   b. psychologist helping a patient
   c. grown-up recalling his past
   d. father objecting to how his children treat him.

2. By saying "Sundays too," the poem shows that all but one of the following is true. Which is false? The father
   a. got up early on weekdays
   b. had Sunday as his day off
   c. fixed the fire every morning
   d. made the boy dress in the cold.

3. *Blue* often describes cold, but this cold is "blueblack." This word is used to show that
   a. it was still dark outside
   b. the house was heated with coal
   c. the shoes took blueblack polish
   d. the father's hands were stained from dirt and labor.

4. The words "No one ever thanked him" in line 5 introduce the speaker's feelings of
   a. anger
   b. regret
   c. hope
   d. trust.

5. The speaker specifically mentions being afraid of
   a. the father
   b. being beaten blueblack
   c. splintering cold
   d. the angers of the house.

6. The father having "cracked hands that ached" implies that he
   a. was old and weak
   b. was too busy to find time for his family
   c. did not care about his appearance
   d. had a hard job doing manual labor.

7. The poem brings out a clear contrast between cold and warmth. List three phrases that plainly show how the father brought warmth to the speaker.

8. By "speaking indifferently to him," the speaker is shown to
   a. take the father's acts for granted
   b. be on the mother's side

c. suffer from poverty and deprivation
d. be purposely mean to the father.

9. Repeating "what did I know" indicates that the speaker
   a. is happy for the chance to repay the father
   b. is a victim of chronic anger because of childhood experiences
   c. realizes the hopelessness of understanding his father's attitude
   d. feels ashamed of not appreciating his father earlier.

10. *Austere* carries with it a sense of coldness as well as severe simplicity. At the end of the poem, the father can be seen as a man who is
    a. cruel, selfish, and heartless
    b. warm and outgoing
    c. indifferent to the welfare of his family
    d. able to express love only in deeds, not words.

In "Those Winter Sundays" Robert Hayden is clearly being serious. By its very nature, a humorous tone is harder to identify, especially when the speaker adopts a mock serious attitude that can fool you into thinking he or she wants to be taken at face value.

Humor is not the same as comedy or being funny. It doesn't necessarily try to make you laugh. By using a humorous tone, a writer plays with words and ideas to show a subject in a fresh and different light.

In the following poem, look for the first word or words that let you know Franklin Pierce Adams isn't being serious about "The Rich Man."

The Rich Man

The rich man has his motor car,
　His country and his town estate.
He smokes a fifty-cent cigar
　And jeers at Fate.

He frivols* through the livelong day.   5
　He knows not Poverty her pinch.
His lot seems light, his heart seems gay.*
　He has a cinch.

Yet though my lamp burns low and dim,
　Though I must slave for livelihood—   10
Think you that I would change with him?
　. . .   !

　　　　　——Franklin Pierce Adams

5. frivol: to play around, to spend one's time having fun. **7. gay**: full of joy.

THINKING IT THROUGH

1. Fill in the last line, using the first two stanzas as a guide. How many words should there be? With what word will it rhyme?

2. Why does the poet wait until the last stanza to introduce a first-person speaker? What words prove that the poet intentionally tried to make the speaker's self-description seem overdrawn?

3. How does the speaker's attitude give clues to the last line? Would the speaker's answer be the same as yours?

4. What are some common ideas about money and happiness that might lead some people to think that the last line doesn't express the right attitude?

5. Although much of the humor is in the last line, what details in the first two stanzas prove Adams isn't seriously describing a rich man's life?

Positive and Negative Words

"Chris is the friendliest person I've ever met."
"Chris is the pushiest person I know."

"Our science teacher sets high standards."
"Our science teacher picks at every little thing."

It's obvious that these paired sentences describe the same people—even the same qualities. Yet they express completely opposite attitudes. When does *friendly* become too friendly—and deserve to be called *pushy*? Where does setting high standards turn into fussiness about unimportant details?

Often, it's a matter of opinion, and the word you choose says it all.

You've seen how words create an image in your mind's eye. In addition, words carry an emotional charge. Although two words may have similar meanings, one may express positive feelings and the other negative ones. **Connotation** means the associated ideas and feelings that a word carries along with its **denotation**, or definition.

EXPERIMENTING WITH WORDS AND IDEAS

1. *Brave* is a positive word, but some words close to it in denotation have connotations less admirable. Read the following synonyms. On a separate piece of paper, mark + if a word is positive, and – if it carries a negative connotation. Use 0 if you are unfamiliar with a word or feel neutral toward it.

reckless	courageous	lion-hearted	daredevil
gallant	tigerish	foolhardy	heroic

2. Working in groups, select one of the following words: *proud*, *thrifty*, *generous*, *peace-loving*, *determined*, *truthful*, *loyal*, or one of your choice describing similar characteristics. List eight to ten words with basically the same meaning that direct you to look at the negative or positive side of the trait you chose. Indicate which have positive, negative, or neutral connotations.

Share your list with class members, and see if they agree with your conclusion.

Since decisions about connotation are based largely on feelings, it's impossible to be wrong. But it is interesting to see how your reaction compares to that of the majority. You'll probably find that most people agree most of the time. To allow for differences of opinion and problems with vocabulary, however, poems generally contain several words that give clues to connotation, not just one.

Two Poems About War

War is a powerful word and, like other words, it can have either positive or negative connotations, depending on the intention of the person using it. As you read the following poems, be alert for connotative clues that guide you to the response sought by each poet.

The Soldier

If I should die, think only this of me:
    That there's some corner of a foreign field
That is forever England. There shall be
    In that rich earth a richer dust concealed;
A dust whom England bore, shaped, made aware,   5
    Gave, once, her flowers to love, her ways to roam,
A body of England's, breathing English air,
    Washed by the rivers, blest by suns of home.
And think, this heart, all evil shed away,
    A pulse in the eternal mind, no less   10
        Gives somewhere back the thoughts by England given;
Her sights and sounds; dreams happy as her day;
And laughter, learnt of friends; and gentleness,
    In hearts at peace, under an English heaven.

——Rupert Brooke

Suicide in the Trenches

I knew a simple soldier boy
Who grinned at life in empty joy,
Slept soundly through the lonesome dark,
And whistled early with the lark.

In winter trenches, cowed* and glum,   5
With crumps* and lice and lack of rum,
He put a bullet through his brain,
No one spoke of him again.

      *   *   *

You smug-faced crowd with kindling* eyes
Who cheer when soldier lads march by,   10
Sneak home and pray you'll never know
The hell where youth and laughter go.

—Siegfried Sassoon

5. cowed: frightened and disheartened. **6. crumps**: bombs, artillery shells.
9. kindling: burning, fiery (pronounced to rhyme with *dwindling*).

COMPARING TWO VIEWS

1. In "The Soldier," the speaker is an English soldier expressing his feelings about dying for his country. Instead of using negative words, what phrases in lines 4, 8, 9, and 10 ask you to think positively of this sacrifice?

2. Line 6 introduces a series of positive things that England gave the soldier. Name at least three.

3. Explain lines 2 and 3. Why would "some corner of a foreign field" be "forever England" if the soldier was a victim of battle? In lines 9 and 10, how would his heart be a "pulse in the eternal mind"?

4. To fit the rest of the poem, why must the phrase "English heaven" mean the sky over his homeland, not heaven "in the eternal mind"?

5. Line 11 speaks of England's being given back what it has given. How does line 14 express the most positive thought possible about the outcome of war?

6. In "Suicide in the Trenches," what is the only piece of information given about the speaker?

7. From the first stanza, list both positive and negative words used to describe the boy and his life. Does the word *simple* lead you to think that he is different from or like most young soldiers? Why?

8. What negative words are used in the second stanza? Explain why "No one spoke of him again."

9. How are both positive and negative words used in the last stanza? By telling the crowd to "sneak" home, how is the speaker saying they ought to feel? Why?

10. Compare the phrase "laughter, learnt of friends" in "The Soldier" with "smug-faced crowd with kindling eyes" in "Suicide in the Trenches." How does each poem bring out a different relationship between a soldier and the folks back home?

EXPRESSING YOUR CONCLUSIONS

Write a composition comparing these two poems and their attitudes toward war, using the following questions to guide your discussion.

1. What contrasting attitudes toward war do these poems reflect?

2. There is no mention of actual battle in "The Soldier" and nothing about a purpose for war in "Suicide in the Trenches." What is the reason for these omissions?

3. Are these attitudes toward war incompatible or do both contain elements of truth? Explain the reasons for your response.

Making Every Word Count

Concerning the use of language, it's been said that, to break the rules successfully, you need to know the reason for the rules and why you're breaking them.

After reading the following, decide what rules of "good" English Theodore Roethke has broken and why.

Child on Top of a Greenhouse

The wind billowing out of the seat of my britches,
My feet crackling splinters of glass and dried putty,
The half-grown chrysanthemums staring up like accusers,
Up through the streaked glass, flashing with sunlight,
A few white clouds all rushing eastward,   5
A line of elms plunging and tossing like horses,
And everyone, everyone pointing up and shouting.

——Theodore Roethke

EXPERIMENTING WITH WORDS AND IDEAS

Did you realize that this poem has no complete subject-verb-object sentence structure? All of the action comes from *-ing* and other verb forms. There are twelve of them in all. List them on a separate sheet of paper.

If this poem were written in standard English, the first sentence might read:

The wind billows out of the seat of my britches.
or
The wind is billowing out of the seat of my britches.

Using these examples as a guide, restate the poem in five or six sentences, using present tense verbs and formal punctuation. You may use simple verbs or the *-ing* forms with *is* or *are* as helpers.

Work from both your own and Roethke's versions to answer the following:

1. What kind of day is it?

2. Why are the flowers "like accusers"?

3. What are some of the things that "everyone" must be shouting?

4. If you were the child on top of the greenhouse, what mixture of emotions might you have? Why?

5. Compare your prose version with the original poem. Which seems to have the most action?

6. Which puts you inside the scene? Why does your choice have more of this effect?

7. What do you think were Roethke's main reasons for breaking the rules?

Learning to Paraphrase

As you've just seen, restating a poem gives you a chance to view it from a different angle and often makes it easier to understand. Because of changes in language, it is also helpful to do this with poetry of the past.

Paraphrasing a poem means to restate it so that the new version runs parallel to the original. To be of value, your rewritten version must make complete sense to you and be in natural-sounding, up-to-date English. Even a bit of slang might not be out of place if it serves to clarify. You need pay no attention to rhythm and rhyme.

For practice, write out a paraphrase of "On Change of Weathers." As you progress, you should make a habit of figuring out a paraphrased version, in your head if not on paper, whenever a passage or poem seems tricky to grasp.

On Change of Weathers

And were it for thy profit, to obtain
All sunshine? No vicissitude* of rain?
Think'st thou that thy laborious plough requires
Not winter frosts as well as summer fires?
There must be both: sometimes these hearts of ours   5
Must have the sweet, the seasonable showers
Of tears; sometimes the frost of chill despair
Makes our desired sunshine seem more fair;
Weathers that most oppose the flesh and blood
Are such as help to make our harvest good.   10
We may not choose, great God: it is thy task;
We know not what to have, nor how to ask.

——Francis Quarles

2. **vicissitude**: change of luck, variation.

Here is a paraphrase of the first four lines.

> And would it be to your advantage to have
> nothing but sunshine? No variety with times of rain?
> Do you believe that you don't need the cold of winter
> as well as the heat of summer to make your plow work?

On a separate sheet of paper, copy these lines or write a variation of your own. Then paraphrase the rest of the poem.

Remember, paraphrase is a tool to help you understand a poem; it is not a substitute for a poem. If the paraphrase is an adequate substitute, then you haven't got much of a poem.

THINKING IT THROUGH

1. It is obvious that the poem is referring to more than the changes of weather that concern a farmer. What is its real subject?

2. What positive and negative words describe the vicissitudes of weather? What positive and negative words describe the vicissitudes of life?

3. What idea does the poem express? After comparing the paraphrase to the original, what, if anything, seems to have been lost by restating the poem?

What Makes a Poem Poetic?

Some people object to poetry because they think of it as nothing but pretty ideas with flowery words and lots of adjectives. As you've seen, poets can write about any subject, and they're more concerned with finding the right word than a pretty one.

In fact, good poetry does not rely on adjectives—not at all. Just like other knowledgeable writers, poets search for precise nouns and strong verbs to carry their meaning.

John Ciardi writes that there is one basic rule by which you can measure the quality of a poem's language: "Count the adjectives and the verbs; good writing (active writing) will almost invariably have more verbs."

Test Ciardi's rule by listing in separate columns all the verbs and adjectives you find in the following poem. You may list descriptive adjectives like *cold* as well as those like *thy* and *that*, which can also be pronouns. Either way, Ciardi's rule should hold true if this is an example of what he calls good writing.

When We Two Parted

When we two parted
  In silence and tears,
Half broken-hearted
  To sever for years,
Pale grew thy cheek and cold,   5
  Colder thy kiss;
Truly that hour foretold
  Sorrow to this.

The dew of the morning
  Sunk chill on my brow—   10
It felt like the warning
  Of what I feel now.
Thy vows are all broken,
  And light* is thy fame;
I hear that name spoken,   15
  And share in its shame.

They name thee before me,
  A knell* to mine ear;
A shudder comes o'er me—
  Why were thou so dear?   20
They know not I knew thee,
  Who knew thee too well:—
Long, long shall I rue* thee,
  Too deeply to tell.

In secret we met—   25
  In silence I grieve
That thy heart could forget,
  Thy spirit deceive.
If I should meet thee
  After long years,   30
How should I greet thee?—
  With silence and tears.

——George Gordon, Lord Byron

---

14. light: a subject for gossip. **18. knell**: a mournful sound. **23. rue**: feel sorrow for.

EXPERIMENTING WITH WORDS AND IDEAS

1. Read the poem over and try to paraphrase it in your head as you go along.

2. In some ways Lord Byron's poem contains ingredients that would be right at home on a soap opera. Write out a synopsis, or condensed version, such as might appear in the television listings of a newspaper. Retell the story behind the poem in no more than four or five sentences of ten to twenty words each.

3. The poem and its synopsis omit many details that would be included if this were a fully developed script for a television soap. List some questions that remain unanswered.

4. Notice that the speaker does not speak face-to-face with the other person but only in thoughts. What lines prove this?

5. If the poem related the juicy items of gossip being passed around instead of simply stating "light is thy fame," would you feel more or less involved and sympathetic with the speaker's situation? Explain your reasoning.

6. If the two should meet again, the speaker plans to greet the other with silence. What are other possibilities for their meeting? What kinds of dialogue can you imagine in such a situation? Why might silence be best and show the most concern?

7. Through their repetition in lines 2 and 32, the words "silence and tears" are shown to be important. Does the poem lead you to think the tears would be an open emotional outburst or inward weeping? What supports your conclusion?

8. Does the speaker still feel love for the other person? What in the poem backs up your opinion?

What Is Poetry About?

"When he looks, he really sees you," someone once said of poet Howard Nemerov.

Going beyond appearances, getting to the heart of its subject, shaping ideas with intent and concentration is what poetry is about. Poetry deals with people's deepest feelings and emotions, but, instead of letting them run wild, it attempts to make them manageable through carefully controlled language. It does not cry out or express self-pity or sound self-important. It is by concentrating on words and trying to get them right that both poet and reader share in the search for and the understanding of the qualities that make people human.

Poets concern themselves with intensely personal subjects, as in "When We Two Parted," or tackle topics like "Truth," as Stephen Crane does next. *Truth* is an abstract word. It names something that can't actually be seen, heard, or identified by means of any of the five senses. Notice how Crane uses concrete words, those that name things which can be perceived by the senses, to clarify two contrasting ideas of truth.

Truth

"Truth," said a traveler,
"Is a rock, a mighty fortress:
Often have I been to it,
Even to its highest tower,
From whence the world looks black."   5

"Truth," said a traveler,
"Is a breath, a wind,
A shadow, a phantom;
Long have I pursued it,
But never have I touched   10
The hem of its garment."

And I believed the second traveler;
For truth was to me
A breath, a wind,
A shadow, a phantom,   15
And never had I touched
The hem of its garment.

                    ——Stephen Crane

FOCUSING IN

Write your answers to the following on a separate sheet of paper.

1. The travelers together use seven concrete nouns to express their ideas of truth. Each of these nouns carries its own image and connotation. Write the letter of the definition on the right that best matches the word from the poem.

   _____ 1. rock

   _____ 2. fortress

   _____ 3. tower

   _____ 4. breath

   _____ 5. wind

   _____ 6. shadow

   _____ 7. phantom

   a. a movement of air that can be felt, not actually seen

   b. representing firmness and solidity

   c. appearing ghostlike and without substance; perhaps a dream or an illusion

   d. offering a place high above others

   e. issuing a set of rules to follow

   f. providing protection, power

   g. no more than a barely heard whisper

   h. seen only by reflection, not in reality

2. The first traveler shows that he views truth as a source of
   a. wisdom
   b. understanding
   c. goodness
   d. power
   e. beauty.

3. In saying "Often have I been to it," the traveler attempts to convince his listener
   a. by giving precise directions
   b. with unsupported evidence or proof
   c. by stating a known fact
   d. with the testimony of those manning the fortress.

4. In lines 10 and 11, "... never have I touched/ The hem of its garment," the second traveler shows awareness that truth has
   a. elements offering power
   b. the appearance of a woman
   c. parts that need to be changed or mended
   d. abstract qualities difficult for the five senses to detect.

5. Instead of seeing truth as distant, lines 10 and 11 make it seem that truth is clearly related to that which is
   a. powerful
   b. stylish
   c. merely common sense
   d. human
   e. pure luck.

6. In the third stanza, the main reason for the speaker's believing the second traveler is
   a. there was more convincing proof
   b. the two agreed
   c. there was less to fear
   d. the second view offered more hope.

7. A humorous comment on life to be drawn from the poem is
   a. people tend to believe those who think the way they do
   b. the world looks blacker the higher you go
   c. some people are never satisfied
   d. travel is not a good teacher.

8. A serious idea in the poem is that truth is
   a. whatever you want it to be
   b. whatever people say when they need a competitive edge
   c. an abstract concept that's useless to consider
   d. impossible to grasp fully but still worth pursuing.

In one of the world's most famous poems, John Keats wrote a description of an ancient Greek vase. After relating his impression as precisely as he could, Keats ended his poem with these lines:

> Beauty is truth, truth beauty.
> That is all ye know on earth,
> And all ye need to know.

How is Keats's idea similar to the second traveler's attitude? How does it differ?

Expressing Your Ideas: Becoming Observant

Observing is one of the most powerful tools a poet has. It allows him or her to concentrate the senses, to separate the valuable from the trivial, to focus with precision.

Boredom may be the result of an unconscious decision that there is nothing worth concentrating on. However, just choosing to observe can make boredom disappear. And observing is a skill that can be developed. Here are two exercises you can use to sharpen your powers of observation.

1. Spend two or three minutes listening to the variety of sounds within your range of hearing. Practice listening at home, in school, outdoors. Pick the place with the most interesting mix of sounds.

Identify three to five different sounds, and describe them as precisely as possible in concrete terms. Answer such questions as What makes the sound? How does it sound? Where does it come from? Which sound is the softest and which the loudest? Which is closest and which farthest away from you?

Write a report of what your listening tells you, presenting it as either prose or poetry. Choose a title for your work that expresses an idea, such as "The Unheard Sounds" or "What Silence Says."

2. Look for three to five objects that you ordinarily wouldn't have noticed. You can do this assignment while you're on your way to school, in class, or at home.

Describe the things you've observed as accurately as possible, in either poetry or prose. Use concrete nouns and precise verbs. Try to make the object you describe stand apart from others like it. If you describe a lamppost or an oak tree, do so in a way that will allow someone to pick out your lamppost or oak tree from all other lampposts or oak trees. Consider such questions as these: Why might you have otherwise overlooked these things? Why are or aren't they really important? You may wish to base your description on a title or topic, such as "Oh Say, Why Didn't I See?" or "After a Closer Look."

Summing Up

Poetry is a concentrated form of writing that requires close attention to the poet's choice of words. By asking yourself why a poet decided on a particular word, you discover important clues to the meaning of the entire poem.

Words are more than just labels for things and ideas. And, your reaction to words is not limited to dictionary definitions. Two words may be very similar in meaning—but cause a very different emotional response.

Poets strive to use words for their fullest effect. They prefer precise nouns and strong, active verbs that state their meaning with exactness. And, although it is often helpful to paraphrase a poem in order to approach its ideas from another angle, remember that the words in the poem have the final say.

Becoming sensitive to the rightness of word choices will help you read with greater understanding and accuracy.

CHAPTER FOUR

Playing with Words, Seriously

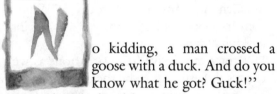

"No kidding, a man crossed a goose with a duck. And do you know what he got? Guck!"

"Honestly now, maybe he crossed a duck with a goose...and got a deuce."

How many kinds of word games can you name? Riddles, puns, crosswords, charades, jokes—people like to play with words.

Did you hear what the doughnut maker said?

"I'm sick and tired of the hole business."
"I can't make enough bread."
"I need to raise more dough."

Those are crumby jokes. You've got a lot of crust to tell them. "Then I'd better wrap this up."

When people say puns like these, which play on double meanings, the punster doesn't expect a surefire laugh. First comes a pause while the pun takes effect. Next follows a groan or a meager chuckle when the listener catches on.

Some might even call puns a form of punishment...but that's enough.

Playing with words does not necessarily mean trying to be outrageously funny. It's often an attempt to put a different twist on words—like putting a spin on a ball—in order to make them worthy of attention.

Much of a poet's work involves playing with words, trying to tease the most from them in different ways. Often "getting the point" is just a matter of seeing how a poet has used a special technique.

57

Irony: The Attraction of Being Opposite

Imagine yourself in the school lunchroom, wearing a brand new sweater. You're nervous because of a report you have to present in the next class. And then you spill a big blob of something bright and juicy, right where it's noticeable.

"Now, wasn't that a clever trick!" you cry.

Why didn't you come right out and say *stupid*? It wasn't pride. It was that *stupid* didn't seem strong enough. You said the opposite of what you meant in order to give your feelings extra emphasis.

That's irony.

Irony means using words to convey the opposite of their usual meaning.

There is always a sense of unexpected reversal in irony. Although sometimes confused with irony, sarcasm is different. It always expresses a determination to "cut someone up" verbally. You can use sarcasm directly by saying "You're so dumb" or indirectly by "You're so clever." But only the second statement is ironical.

You might even try to cheer up a glum friend by saying, "What puts you in such a sunny mood today?" Why might it be better to start the conversation ironically, instead of making a comment about your friend's looking "down"?

Irony can derive from situations as well as words. In an ironic situation, the result turns out to be the opposite of what you would expect. Here's one:

A sharpshooter tries to show off his fancy gun handling and shoots himself in the toe.

That's irony. It might even be funny, if he only nicked the tip of his boot.

Be careful not to confuse irony with coincidence. If two women wear identical dresses to a party, that's coincidence. *Coincidence* is an odd pairing of events that unexpectedly happen at the same time, apparently by chance.

Irony, on the other hand, contains a twist of fate, and the unexpected outcome often seems like a trick of poetic justice.

EXPERIMENTING WITH WORDS AND IDEAS

1. Compare the following situations. Which is coincidence and which is situation irony? How do you know?

    On his first day in Paris, a traveler runs into someone who lives on the same street in his hometown in the United States.

    A man goes to Paris wearing a disguise and using an assumed name. When registering at the hotel, someone from his hometown greets him by his real name.

2. Writers often choose names to create just the right impression of their characters. Names can also be a clue to someone's nationality or to the story's setting.

Uriah Heap and Nick Carraway are two fictional characters. Basing your reaction solely on the names, which seems more likeable?

From the following names, decide which country each pair comes from.

a. Gretchen and Hans
b. Pedro and Juan
c. Hounan and Ahmad

d. Pierre and Yvonne
e. Chang and Lin
f. Olga and Boris

You can also ''tell time'' by using names. For example, few people today have first names like Silas, Mehitabel, or Hector. What kinds of names would you invent or suggest for a science fiction or futuristic narrative?

The character in the following poem is named ''Ozymandias.'' What ideas about place and person do you associate with such a name? Do you think it's a real name or an invented one? Do you think Ozymandias would be from one of the countries you named in activity 2? Why or why not? Check your guesses as you read.

Ozymandias

I met a traveler from an antique land,
Who said: Two vast and trunkless* legs of stone
Stand in the desert. Near them, on the sand,
Half sunk, a shattered visage* lies, whose frown,
And wrinkled lip, and sneer of cold command,   5
Tell that its sculptor well those passions read,
Which yet survive, stamped on these lifeless things,
The hand that mocked* them, and the heart that fed:
And on the pedestal these words appear:
"My name is Ozymandias, King of Kings: 10
Look on my works, ye Mighty, and despair!"
Nothing beside remains. Round the decay
Of that colossal wreck, boundless and bare
The lone and level sands stretch far away.

—Percy Bysshe Shelley

2. trunkless: without a body or torso. **4. visage:** face. **8. mocked:** made; imitated.

THINKING IT THROUGH

1. "Ozymandias" serves as a perfect example of irony. The inscription on the pedestal said, "Look on my works." What must Ozymandias have thought visitors would see? Explain.

2. Judging by the inscription given in lines 10–11, how did the "King of Kings" expect future generations to feel after looking at his colossal statue? Why did he expect the "Mighty" to react this way?

3. What does the traveler report that the statue actually looked like at the time he saw it?

4. What words or phrases does the poet use to create a positive or negative attitude toward Ozymandias? What kind of ruler must he have been?

5. Lines 6 and 7 refer to "passions. . .which yet survive." Consider such traits as greed, cruelty, arrogance, and thirst for power. How does the poem show that Ozymandias possessed these traits? Have you evidence of their surviving in certain world leaders of today?

6. What clues in the poem show the sculptor's attitude toward his subject?

7. How would it change the reader's reaction to the poem if the first lines were changed to read as follows:

    > I was a traveler in an antique land,
    > And there two vast and trunkless legs of stone
    > Stand in the desert. . .

8. How much information is given about the land that Ozymandias ruled? In what part of the world was it? What does the poem say remains of it today? Do you thing it was real or imaginary? Why or why not?

9. What is the irony, the difference between what Ozymandias expected and what really happened? Would you call it a trick of fate that he deserved? Explain.

10. How are the words "King of Kings" also ironical? What is the poet's attitude toward pride and vanity? How do you know?

The Serious Side of Humor

Satire is writing that makes fun of a serious situation. What serious truth is Shelley addressing in "Ozymandias"?

Sometimes, by refusing to take the accepted viewpoint or say the accepted thing, a poet forces the reader to look at a situation in a new light. In the following poem, Alice Walker deals with a serious problem ironically, addressing her reader as though she were talking of etiquette or good manners.

Suicide

First, suicide notes should be
(not long) but written
second,
all suicide notes
should be signed   5
in blood
by hand
and to the point—
the point of being, perhaps
that there is none.   10
Thirdly, if it is the thought
of rest that
fascinates
laziness should be admitted
in the clearest terms.   15
Then, all things done
ask those outraged
consider their happiest
summer
& tell if the days it   20
adds up to
is one.

——Alice Walker

T H I N K I N G   I T   T H R O U G H

1. Alice Walker's poem ''Suicide'' is divided into four parts, starting as if to give one kind of advice and progressing to another. What do the first seven lines purport to help with? What are five pieces of advice they offer? How do you know Walker can't be serious?

2. Lines 8 and 9 use repetition to call attention to an important ''point,'' with each use of that word having a slightly different focus. The first use means ''said with no wasted words.''

   How would you define *point* as used in line 9? Restate lines 9 and 10 so that the meaning is clearer, beginning, ''Perhaps the point is that . . . .'' Why do you think the poet used the word *perhaps* instead of being more direct?

3. In lines 11–13, what reason does Walker give for someone's contemplating suicide?

   Why do you think Walker chose *rest* as an example? What advice does she give in lines 14–15? How is this a change from the type of advice she pretended to give in the first nine lines?

4. "Then" in line 16 begins the final section. Sticking with the words in the poem, what must be meant by "all things done"? *Outraged* means "angered, offended, made resentful." Who must Walker mean by "those [who are] outraged"?

5. Lines 17–22 have several words omitted but understood. What is the subject of the verb *ask*? What word would you supply before *consider* and *tell*? What are "those outraged" to do? What must Walker assume the answer will be, "one" or "more than one"? How do you know?

6. If Walker's advice were stated directly, how would it have been given? What do you think was her purpose in stating it ironically instead?

What's Really Being Said?

What was the Battle of Blenheim? As you'll discover, you needn't really know to understand the following poem. But from the place name plus the characters' names of Kaspar, Peterkin, and Wilhelmine, where do you think the setting might be?

Even though this narrative poem has the singsong sound of a nursery tale, you'll find the light touch of its humor carries a strong dose of satire. Watch to see how the poet accomplishes this feat through the use of irony and repetition.

The Battle of Blenheim

It was a summer evening;
  Old Kaspar's work was done,
And he before his cottage door
  Was sitting in the sun;
And by him sported on the green   5
His little grandchild Wilhelmine.

She saw her brother Peterkin
  Roll something large and round
Which he beside the rivulet*
  In playing there had found.   10
He came to ask what he had found,
That was so large, and smooth, and round.

9. **rivulet:** small stream or brook.

Old Kaspar took it from the boy,
  Who stood expectant by;
And then the old man shook his head,   15
  And with a natural sigh,
" 'Tis some poor fellow's skull," said he,
"Who fell in the great victory.

"I find them in the garden,
  For there's many here about;   20
And often, when I go to plow,
  The plowshare turns them out;
For many thousand men," said he,
"Were slain in that great victory."

"Now tell us what 'twas all about,"   25
  Young Peterkin, he cries;
And little Wilhelmine looks up
  With wonder-waiting eyes;
"Now tell us all about the war,
And what they fought each other for."   30

"It was the English," Kaspar cried,
  "Who put the French to rout;*
But what they fought each other for,
  I could not well make out;
But everybody said," quoth* he,   35
"That 'twas a famous victory.

"My father lived at Blenheim then,
  Yon little stream hard by;
They burnt his dwelling to the ground,
  And he was forced to fly;   40
So with his wife and child he fled,
Nor had he where to rest his head.

"With fire and sword the country round
  Was wasted far and wide,
And many a childing mother then,   45
  And new-born baby, died;
But things like that, you know, must be
At every famous victory.

"They say it was a shocking sight
  After the field was won;   50
For many thousand bodies here
  Lay rotting in the sun;
But things like that, you know, must be
After a famous victory.

(continued on next page)

"Great praise the Duke of Marlbro' won,   55
  And our good Prince Eugene."
"Why, 'twas a very wicked thing!"
  Said little Wilhelmine.
"Nay, nay, my little girl," quoth he;
"It was a famous victory.   60

"And everybody praised the Duke
  Who this great fight did win."
"But what good came of it at last?"
  Quoth little Peterkin.
"Why, that I cannot tell," said he;   65
"But 'twas a famous victory."

——Robert Southey

32. rout: a disorderly flight or retreat. **35. quoth:** said.

FOCUSING IN

1. What is the "large, smooth, and round" object that Peterkin was innocently playing with in the poem "The Battle of Blenheim"? In line 24, what seems ironical about calling the battle a "great victory," as Kaspar does for a second time?

2. In line 30, Wilhelmine asks her grandfather to tell her and her brother why the men were fighting. Does Kaspar really answer her in stanza 6?

3. What does Kaspar know about the reason for the fight? What reason does he have for calling it "a famous victory"? Is it a good reason?

THINKING IT THROUGH

1. In stanzas 7, 8, and 9 (beginning with the line "My father lived at Blenheim then" on page 63), Kaspar gives his grandchildren some hard evidence about what actually happened at the battle. What are three examples?

2. The words "famous victory" show the power of repetition to create irony. Why do the words become more and more ironical? What attitude is created toward Kaspar as a result of this repetition? Why is it the easy way out to claim "it was a famous victory"?

3. What line in stanza 10 sums up the attitude the poet creates toward the battle?

4. What answer does the poem lead you to believe would be best in response to Peterkin's question, "What good came of it?"

5. Did Southey intend this satire to apply only to the Battle of Blenheim or to wars in general? What in the poem makes you think so?

6. How would you put Southey's satirical comment if you stated it in a straightforward manner?

7. What advantages did Southey gain by telling the story as he did, in a simple way with children and an old man as the characters?

Ambiguity: You Can Have It Both Ways

"Do you want this written in pencil or pen?"
"Yes."
"Would you like me to give you a clip?"
"No.
"Did you bring me my wire?"
"Huh?"

Without more data, you can't tell what these three questions are about. All are ambiguous. They are capable of being taken in more than one way.

Ambiguity is different from punning. A pun also has a double meaning, but one definition always fits more sensibly with the rest of the statement.

An ambiguous statement offers no clues to clear up the confusion, and, when it occurs by mistake, ambiguity can cause serious misunderstandings. However, it can be used intentionally, as John Suckling does in the following poem. As you read it, see how the poet plays on the ambiguity of the word *constant*. Bear in mind the word's two meanings: *constant* can mean "faithful, loyal, and steadfast" or "occurring repeatedly."

The Constant Lover

Out upon it,* I have loved
  Three whole days together!
And am like* to love three more,
  If it prove fair weather.

Time shall molt* away his wings   5
  Ere* he shall discover
In the whole wide world again
  Such a constant lover.

But the spite* on't is, no praise
  Is due at all to me;   10
Love with me had made no stays,
  Had it any been but she.

Had it any been but she,
  And that very face,
There had been at least ere this   15
  A dozen dozen in her place.

———Sir John Suckling

1. Out upon it: an expression of disgust directed at an accuser. **3. like:** likely.
5. molt: shed, lose. **6. ere:** before. **9. spite:** shame, unfortunate part.

F O C U S I N G   I N

Answer the following on a separate sheet of paper. Be prepared to explain your choices.

1. The speaker in the poem should be taken to be
   a. John Suckling
   b. the constant lover
   c. a critic
   d. a broken-hearted suitor.

2. By the expression of disgust, the speaker shows that someone has probably
   a. accused him of being fickle
   b. criticized him for being a coward
   c. given him only three days to mend his ways
   d. challenged him to a duel.

3. The speaker claims to have loved "three whole days together" to
   a. show he can have any girl he wants
   b. prove his constancy
   c. make the reader understand his heartbreak
   d. show there's no cause for alarm.

4. Suckling's having the speaker say he has loved "three whole days together" is an example of
   a. a pun
   b. ambiguity
   c. connotation
   d. irony.

5. In stanza two, the speaker implies he is
   a. wasting his time
   b. seeking to discover a constant lover
   c. the world's most faithful lover
   d. ready to shed his fickle ways.

6. The total length of time that the speaker can imagine himself loving one woman is
   a. a dozen years
   b. a lifetime
   c. till Time molts away his wings
   d. six days.

7. By having the speaker say, "no praise/ Is due at all to me," the poet is poking fun at
   a. quickness to complain
   b. blind stubbornness
   c. false modesty
   d. utter foolishness.

8. According to the speaker, if it hadn't been for the special woman and her face, how many women would he have loved during the time he had been true to her?
   a. 6
   b. 12
   c. 24
   d. 144.

9. Which definition best fits the word *constant* as used in this poem?
   a. loyal and faithful
   b. repeatedly changing
   c. neither definition
   d. both definitions, depending on the viewpoint.

10. The poet Suckling invites the reader to
    a. be sharply critical of the speaker
    b. feel the speaker has been badly wronged
    c. be angered by the injustice in the world
    d. be amused but aware of the speaker's self-deception.

Metaphor: Bringing Ideas into Clearer View

In his poem "Truth," Stephen Crane could have written, "Truth is something that you sometimes believe you see, but you can't always be sure whether it's really there or just a product of your imagination."

Instead, he wrote, "Truth is a phantom."

He saved all those words and let you see his meaning more clearly and easily than if he'd tried to tell you.

"Truth is a phantom" is an example of *metaphor*, a comparison that asks you to see the similarities between two things that at first glance seem unlike one another. Its purpose is to put the first in sharper focus by inviting you to see the qualities it shares with the second.

In reading poetry, you need not go searching for metaphors. In fact, the poet more likely wants them to come looking for you—to create a clearer picture for more accurate reading.

If Crane had written, "Truth is like a phantom," this would still be a metaphor, but a slightly different type called a *simile*: an indirect comparison introduced by *like* or *as*.

Many of the poems you've already read contain metaphors and similes. You don't have to be able to name a metaphor to understand it. Like all specialized subjects, poetry has its own technical language. Knowing terminology can be helpful when it provides verbal shortcuts to meaningful discussion.

As you develop sensitivity in reading, you'll discover that the more you read poetry, the more you'll find within each poem you encounter. As you become more aware of metaphors, you'll discover how carefully a poet seeks exactly the right comparison to plant the sought-after image in your mind.

Look again at "Truth" on page 52 and ask yourself the reasons for its metaphors.

Why is truth like a fortress? Like a shadow?

Of course, these are somewhat like riddles, but they're the poet's way of letting you see—and feel—the idea for yourself.

The use of metaphors is another example of how writers expect their readers to take an active part in the reading game.

How Do Poets Use Metaphor?

Sometimes metaphors help create the setting, as in the narrative poem "The Highwayman," by Alfred Noyes. Throughout the long poem (only the first stanza is given here), metaphors not only give a picture of the scene but also foreshadow, or offer clues about, how the poem will develop.

The Highwayman

The wind was a torrent* of darkness among the gusty trees,
The moon was a ghostly galleon* tossed upon cloudy seas,
The road was a ribbon of moonlight over the purple moor,*
And the highwayman came riding—
   Riding—riding—   5
The highwayman can riding, up to the old inn-door.

—Alfred Noyes

Highwayman: a robber who holds up travelers. **1. torrent:** a violent rush.
2. galleon: a three-masted sailing ship. **3. moor:** open expanse of land often overgrown with heather, found in Scotland and England.

THINKING IT THROUGH

1. How do clouds make the moon look like a "ghostly galleon"?

2. How does this metaphor show you the historical period in which the poem is set?

3. What hint does the word *ghostly* give you about the story this poem tells?

4. What kind of picture does "ribbon of moonlight" create? Does this metaphor best fit a spooky, romantic, or funny tale? Why?

5. Like Johnie Armstrong, the highwayman is wanted by the king's men. He is a heroic figure who risks his freedom to see Bess, the girl he loves. Soldiers hold her hostage to trap him. From the opening stanza would you guess the poem ends happily or unhappily? How do metaphors serve as clues?

Your teacher may ask a student to find this narrative poem and share it with everyone.

Metaphors Express a Key Idea

What would it mean if you said that someone liked to "take the truth and stand it on its head"? Would that be the same thing as lying? In the first two stanzas from the following poem, "Exaggerator," notice how poet Mark Van Doren uses metaphors and similes to express how someone who exaggerates feels about his wild stories.

Exaggerator

The truth for him was like a tree,
Was like a funnel; like a fan;
Like any point from which a cone
Spreads upside down until the span*
From base to base across the top   5
Cannot be guessed by any man.

The truth for him was not the seed,
Was not the apex,* handle, spout;
Was not the particle or germ,
Or what grew thence* so wild and stout;   10
Was not the great, the upper end.
It was the joy of starting out...

——Mark Van Doren

4. span: the distance. **8. apex:** point, peak. **10. thence:** from there.

THINKING IT THROUGH

1. Draw rough sketches of a tree, a funnel, a fan, and a cone all turned upside down. According to the poem, at what spot on each object would you find the truth?

2. How do these sketches illustrate an exaggeration? If someone loves to exaggerate, what about his story "cannot be guessed by any man"?

3. The second stanza uses metaphors in some ways both similar to and different from the way Stephen Crane uses them. By using "not," what is Van Doren emphasizing?

4. What six objects does Van Doren compare to truth in stanza 2? What two seem different from the rest? How are they different? Why do the others express a similar idea?

5. Compare the first lines of each stanza. What do their metaphors have to do with one another? How does comparing them help explain line 10? What grew so "wild and stout," metaphorically speaking?

6. What did Van Doren mean by saying the Exaggerator was not concerned with "the great, the upper end"? Did he want to gain some advantage or financial return for his exaggeration? Support your conclusion.

7. What is "the joy of starting out"? Can you understand how the Exaggerator felt? Would you like to have his ability? Why or why not?

Metaphors Bring Out the Feeling

In "Pretty Words," Elinor Wylie uses similes to compare words to different creatures. Notice how Wylie appeals to the five senses through her carefully chosen metaphors. Also, be alert to see whether Wylie truly believes that poetry is just pretty words...or is there a bit of a zinger waiting?

Pretty Words

Poets make pets of pretty, docile* words:
I love smooth words, like gold-enameled fish
Which circle slowly with a silken swish,
And tender ones, like down-feathered birds;
Words shy and dappled,* deep-eyed deer in herds,   5
Come to my hand, and playful if I wish,
Or purring softly at a silver dish,
Blue Persian kitten, fed on cream and curds.*

I love bright words, words up and singing early;
Words that are luminous in the dark, and sing;   10
Warm lazy words, white cattle under trees;
I love words opalescent,* cool, and pearly,
Like midsummer moths, and honeyed words like bees,
Gilded and sticky, with a little sting.

——Elinor Wylie

1. docile: tame. **5. dappled:** spotted. **8. curds:** milk product. **12. opalescent:** displaying lustrous colors.

THINKING IT THROUGH

1. What lines and phrases plainly express the idea that poets enjoy playing with words?

2. From her choice of similes, do you think Wylie likes words that are totally tame? Support your answer.

3. What descriptive words does Wylie use to appeal to the sense of sight? Of hearing? Of touch? Of taste?

4. Compare the last two lines with the title. What possible contradiction do you see? What do you think Wylie means by saying she loves words "with a little sting"? How can you play with words to make them have "a little sting"?

5. In writing this poem, what words and phrases do you think Wylie must have especially enjoyed finding or taming or using because they seemed just right?

EXPERIMENTING WITH WORDS AND IDEAS

You probably use metaphors more than you think, often without recognizing them. Many of the best-known proverbs, such as "Don't put all your eggs in one basket," are really metaphorical.

Every time you say something is "as light as a feather," you've used a simile. Sayings like these are comfortable and handy. Yet poets aren't likely to "make pets" of such familiar old sayings, which are considered clichés, or overworked expressions. They're all right for everyday speech, but you should avoid them when you want to use "bright words," "playful" words, and "words . . . with a little sting."

Working in groups, read over the following list of sayings. The origins of many stretch back in time, when life was different from today. Choose at least eight examples. First, explain what each means in straightforward terms. Then see if you can devise a new version that expresses the same idea but is brought up-to-date with a new comparison.

Be prepared to present your ideas to the rest of the class and compare your variations.

1. The early bird gets the worm.

2. A watched pot never boils.

3. It's like looking for a needle in a haystack.

4. Every cloud has a silver lining.

5. It was raining cats and dogs.

6. A bird in the hand is worth two in the bush.

7. It's always darkest before dawn.

8. Too many cooks spoil the broth.

9. Don't lock the barn after the horse is stolen.

10. You look like the cat that swallowed the canary.

11. He's a chip off the old block.

12. She's a carbon copy of her mother.

13. It's a piece of cake!

14. She's sharp as a tack.

15. He's smart as a whip.

16. She's crazy like a fox.

Playing with Words to Manipulate

Sometimes words sound so mighty and important that the sound gets in the way of their meaning. Saying "The plan was a catastrophe" sounds far worse than saying it was a flop, even though the result was the same.

Advertisers take advantage of the sounds of words by declaring that their sales are "stupendous" and "spectacular" even if the money you save is hardly worth bragging about.

Carl Sandburg writes about this and other qualities of words in his poem, "Threes."

Threes

I was a boy when I heard three red words
a thousand Frenchmen died in the street
for: Liberty, Equality, Fraternity—I asked
why men die for words.

I was older: men with mustaches, sideburns,   5
lilacs, told me the high golden words are:
Mother, Home, and Heaven—other older men with
face decorations said: God, Duty, Immortality
—they sang these threes slow from deep lungs.

Years ticked off their say-so on the great clocks   10
of doom and damnation, soup and nuts: meteors flashed
their say-so: and out of great Russia came three
dusky syllables workmen took guns and went out to die
for: Bread, Peace, Land.

And I met a marine of the U.S.A., a leatherneck with   15
a girl on his knee for a memory in ports circling the
earth and he said: Tell me how to say three things
and I always get by—gimme a plate of ham and eggs—
how much?—and—do you love me, kid?

——Carl Sandburg

FOCUSING IN

Answer the following on a separate sheet of paper.

1. In stanza 1 the words *Liberty*, *Equality*, and *Fraternity* are examples of
   a. abstract words
   b. concrete words
   c. metaphors
   d. similes
   e. exaggerations.

2. Sandburg calls these words *red* to indicate
   a. a blaze of glory
   b. aflame with rage and anger
   c. stirring, yet spilling blood
   d. a warning
   e. the color of French uniforms.

3. The number "a thousand" in line 2 is probably
   a. an exaggeration
   b. an educated guess
   c. what the speaker saw on the general's official report
   d. the boy's guess, which could be low.

4. By asking why men die for words, the speaker shows himself to be
   a. illogical
   b. stupid
   c. sarcastic
   d. thoughtful
   e. joking.

5. In lines 5 and 6, *lilacs* does not fit with *mustaches* and *sideburns* but completes a mental picture of
   a. Mother
   b. Home
   c. Heaven
   d. God
   e. Duty
   f. Immortality.

6. *Mother*, *Home*, and *Heaven* can be considered "high golden words" because they are
   a. symbols of wealth
   b. flashy but empty of value
   c. sought-after and treasured
   d. not solid or attainable.

7. The three words that were the slogan of "other older men" showed that they were
   a. greedier
   b. looking beyond their earthly lives
   c. most interested in the younger generation
   d. more patriotic than the younger men.

8. By following "doom and damnation" with "soup and nuts" in line 11, Sandburg tries to show that time's passage includes
   a. wars and disasters
   b. little of concern to common people
   c. a continual decline to destruction
   d. both the terrible and the commonplace.

9. The single-syllable words of the Russian workmen were called "dusky" to describe
   a. their aims in contrast to "high golden" ideals
   b. the chill of the Russian winters
   c. the darkness inside a typical Russian coal mine
   d. the color of their bread and land.

10. Which is the abstract word in the "Threes" of the Russian Revolution? What word or words in line 13 make its use seem ironical?

11. In stanza 4, the marine's three things show him to be
   a. an ordinary person
   b. a great hero
   c. an underprivileged boy
   d. a well-informed patriot
   e. a victim of propaganda.

12. Which of the following conclusions can be drawn from the last stanza? The marine
   a. was behaving unpatriotically
   b. needed no slogans to support freedom
   c. did not care about mother, home, or heaven
   d. did not deserve the benefits bestowed by America.

EXPERIMENTING WITH WORDS AND IDEAS

1. How can humor be serious? Alice Walker, Percy Bysshe Shelley, and Robert Southey each show how in their poems in this chapter. Choose one of the topics they satirized, and write a composition of three to five paragraphs explaining how the poem showed the serious side of the topic using techniques of humor.

   Be sure to include the title and author, along with at least three examples from the work.

2. How do you express an abstract idea in concrete terms? Both Stephen Crane and Mark Van Doren took on the challenge in their poems concerning truth.

   See what you can do with an abstract idea. You may select one of the words in Carl Sandburg's "Threes," such as *liberty*, *equality*, *duty*, or *peace*, or choose one of your own, such as *loyalty* or *trust*. Write concrete metaphors that express your ideas and feelings toward the word. Look for five different comparisons, and don't settle for fewer—thinking about words, playing with them, and concentrating on an idea will bring results.

   Write your metaphors in either poetic form or prose.

On Your Own: Keeping a Poetry Notebook

A poem speaks for the poet and tries to speak to everyone who reads it. But it also has something personal to say.

What do you see, and what does a poem say to you? Begin keeping a notebook recording your reactions to poems you encounter. At first your notebook may contain mostly questions, but as you progress, you'll find more and more to comment on. On Your Own activities in the following chapters of this book offer you opportunities to write your personal reactions to poetry in your notebook.

Set up your notebook as a double-entry log containing facts, poetic devices, and interpretations—as well as your own impressions, feelings, and whatever arouses your curiosity. On the left side, write the heading *Points to Note*.

> Include: Key quotes, literary devices, vocabulary, features that need exploration or explanation, special use of language, and lines or phrases that need paraphrasing. Be sure to indicate line or stanza.

On the right side, under the heading *Personally Speaking,*

> Include: Your reaction to quoted words and phrases, questions you have for the poet, ideas you especially like or dislike, the feelings you get from certain words or lines, where you think the poem is heading, how the poem relates to you, what you understand or don't understand—any impression that comes to mind as you read a poem.

Begin by copying this poem into your notebook. It will help you get started, and you can use your notes on it later for reference.

Escape

I never hear the word "escape"
Without a quicker blood,
A sudden expectation,
A flying attitude!

I never hear of prisons broad   5
By soldiers battered down,
But I tug childish at my bars
Only to fail again!

——Emily Dickinson

Summing Up

Play is a way of exploring, and poets play with words to discover new ideas in them. The more you understand about the techniques writers use to explore the possibilities of language, the better prepared you are to meet poetry on its own terms, and the better equipped to conduct some explorations of your own.

To be a good reader of poetry, you must be ready to jump into the game and catch the poet's use of puns or ambiguity, metaphors or irony. Knowing the names of writing techniques helps you achieve the full measure of understanding that comes from being alert to their use.

CHAPTER FIVE

More Than Meets the Eye

No matter when it was written, no matter where its author comes from, good literature contains ideas and emotions that you can recognize as common to yourself and to people everywhere.

Poetry proves that you are not alone. There are others with you, all trying to puzzle out and define what it means to be alive and human.

Seeing with the Mind's Eye

Even though a poem is told in first person, be careful not to confuse speaker and poet. By adopting a persona, a poet can take a fresh look at feelings everyone shares—for his or her own enlightenment as well as a reader's.

You can do the same. Try to get inside the poem and gain a new perspective on universal feelings by seeing through the speaker's eyes.

William Stafford called the following poem "Thinking for Berky." How does this express an idea different from "Thinking *about* Berky"?

Thinking for Berky

In the late night listening from bed
I have joined the ambulance or the patrol
screaming toward some drama, the kind of end
that Berky must have some day, if she isn't dead.
The wildest of all, the father and mother cruel,
farming out there beyond the old stone quarry
where highschool lovers parked their lurching cars,
Berky learned to love in that dark school.

(continued on next page)

79

Early her face was turned away from home
toward any hardworking place; but still her soul   10
with terrible things to do, was alive, looking out
for the rescue that—surely, some day—would have to come.

Windiest nights, Berky, I have thought for you,
and no matter how lucky I've been I've touched wood.
There are things not solved in our town though tomorrow came: 15
there are things time passing can never make come true.

We live in an occupied country, misunderstood;
justice will take us millions of intricate* moves.
Sirens will hunt down Berky, you survivors in your beds
listening through the night, so far and good.   20

—William Stafford

18. intricate: complicated, full of puzzling details.

FOCUSING IN

Write your answers on a separate sheet of paper. Be prepared to cite lines from the poem to back up your choices.

1. True or false? The poem gives no factual clues to the speaker's identity.

2. True or false? The speaker last saw Berky when she was a student at the local high school.

3. True or false? The speaker has no idea where Berky is or even whether she is still living.

4. In the first stanza, a word related to the idea of thinking "for" Berky is the verb
   a. *joined*
   b. *screaming*
   c. *parked*
   d. *learned*

5. To the speaker, sirens symbolize
   a. hope for law and order
   b. thrills and excitement
   c. the probable ill fate of Berky
   d. Berky's getting the punishment she deserves.

6. List two factual details about where Berky's home was and how her parents earned their living.

7. Line 9 states, "Early her face was turned away from home." What word in line 5 explains what she wanted to escape?

8. "That dark school" where Berky learned to love must have been
   a. prison
   b. her home
   c. the local high school
   d. the place where lovers parked.

9. The poem states that Berky's "face was turned away from home [and] toward any hardworking place." This characterizes her as lazy and unwilling to help herself out of poverty and bad surroundings—true or false?

10. Lines 11 and 12 make it seem that Berky
    a. cared for no one and nothing
    b. still hoped for a better life
    c. thought jail was an improvement over home
    d. felt that the world owed her a living.

11. Stanza 3 shows that the speaker believes the main factor causing Berky's wild and desperate life is
    a. luck
    b. time
    c. society
    d. her bad behavior.

12. The speaker uses "we" in line 17 to show that he also
    a. counts on the passage of time
    b. is eager to escape from home
    c. is misunderstood
    d. continues to be hopeful.

13. True or false? After the sirens hunt down Berky, the speaker will find it easier to forget her.

14. True or false? By writing "you survivors in your beds listening," the speaker implies everyone should be thinking for Berky and others like her.

15. The words "occupied country" and "survivors" make it seem that the speaker considers Berky
    a. an enemy
    b. a friend
    c. a freedom fighter
    d. a victim.

Comparing Ideas

After reading ''Thinking for Berky,'' how would you explain Stafford's choice of the word *for* in the title?

A famous poet of the seventeenth century, John Donne wrote these lines about the ringing of church bells for a funeral:

> And therefore never send to know
> for whom the bell tolls; it tolls for thee.

In what ways are a tolling bell and a siren alike? Does Donne express an idea similar to the one in ''Thinking for Berky''? What supports your conclusion?

Through Another's Eyes

Sara Teasdale's ''Barter'' asks you to look at life from an entirely different viewpoint. The word *barter* means ''exchanging goods and services without using money.'' See how the first two lines give you a direct clue to the kinds of things that life has to sell. Note what each one is and how it fits logically with the others.

The title also directs you to expect that something must be offered in exchange. Watch for this second element, necessary to complete the barter, and decide whether the poem supports the trade as being a fair one.

Barter

> Life has loveliness to sell
>   All beautiful and splendid things,
> Blue waves whitened on a cliff,
>   Soaring fire that sways and sings,
> And children's faces looking up,   5
> Holding wonder like a cup.
>
> Life has loveliness to sell,
>   Music like a curve of gold,
> Scent of pine trees in the rain,
>   Eyes that love you, arms that hold,   10
> And for your spirit's still* delight,
> Holy thoughts that star the night.

Spend all you have for loveliness,
   Buy it and never count the cost;
For one white singing hour of peace   15
   Count many a year of strife* well lost,
And for a breath of ecstasy*
Give all you have been, or could be.

—Sara Teasdale

11. still: calm, undisturbed. **16. strife:** struggle, great effort. **17. ecstasy:** pure and utter joy.

THINKING IT THROUGH

1. What "beautiful and splendid things" does life have to sell? List five examples that Teasdale gives in the first ten lines.

2. Each of these examples represents a category of similar things. Name one or two additional items to fit each group, and choose a term that describes each category.

3. How do lines 11 and 12 introduce an idea that differs from the items previously listed?

4. Where does Teasdale introduce the full terms of the barter? What three lines directly tell the price you should be willing to pay for life's loveliness and joy? Write the key words from these lines.

5. Teasdale doesn't include anything that can be bought with money. What then does she actually mean for you to "spend"?

6. In spite of the apparent differences between Teasdale's and Stafford's poems, do you think Berky would agree with the idea of "spend[ing] all you have for loveliness"? Use lines from both poems to support your answer.

The Real Subject

At the outset, "The First Snow-Fall" seems purely descriptive. Watch for the first clues to something more.

A poem's purpose is easier to understand when you discover how its ideas are organized. "The First Snow-Fall" divides naturally into three sections, each with a different focus. When you have finished reading the poem on the next two pages, decide which stanzas belong together and why.

The First Snow-Fall

The snow had begun in the gloaming,*
  And busily all the night
Had been heaping field and highway
  With a silence deep and white.

Every pine and fir and hemlock   5
  Wore ermine too dear for an earl,
And the poorest twig on the elm-tree
  Was ridged inch deep with pearl.

From sheds new-roofed with Carrara*
  Came Chanticleer's* muffled crow,   10
The stiff rails softened to swan's-down,*
  And still fluttered down the snow.

I stood and watched by the window
  The noiseless work of the sky,
And the sudden flurries of snow-birds,   15
  Like brown leaves whirling by.

I thought of a mound in sweet Auburn*
  Where a little headstone stood;
How the flakes were folding it gently,
  As did robins the babes in the wood.   20

Again I looked at the snow-fall,
  And thought of the leaden sky
That arched o'er our first great sorrow
  When that mound was heaped so high.

I remembered the gradual patience   25
  That fell from the cloud like snow,
Flake by flake, healing and hiding
  The scar that renewed our woe.

And again to the child I whispered,
  "The snow that husheth all,   30
Darling, the merciful Father
  Alone can make it fall!"

---

1. gloaming: early dusk, twilight. **9. Carrara:** a type of white marble.
10. Chanticleer: a rooster. **11. swan's-down:** soft feathers of a swan.
17. Auburn: name of a town.

Then, with eyes that saw not, I kissed her,
And she, kissing back, could not know
That *my* kiss was given to her sister,   35
Folded close under deepening snow.

——James Russell Lowell

FOCUSING IN

1. Name three metaphors that compare the change brought by the snow to riches. Why is each appropriate?

2. Name two harsher things softened by the snow.

3. As the speaker watches the snow, what past event does he remember?

4. What words express the depth and extent of his feelings? Find at least two examples, and explain what they reveal.

5. What healed and hid "the scar that renewed our woe"? Does this mean that the scar is the physical mound or the memory. Explain.

6. As the speaker kisses his daughter, what does he think?

7. How do the speaker's words and action show him concerned about and sensitive to the feelings of the child with him?

8. In stanza 1 the poem speaks of deep silence and in stanza 4 of "the noiseless work of the sky." How does this fit in with the words spoken to the child in lines 30–32?

9. What does the thought of "her sister,/ Folded close under deepening snow" mean to the speaker?

10. The poet's 14-month-old daughter died in March, and another daughter was born the following September. Even though Lowell's life closely followed that of the speaker, what ideas in this poem go beyond the strictly personal?

11. What is the organization of the poem? What is the purpose of each set of stanzas? How does this clarify the underlying ideas?

Expressing Yourself

Discuss one of the following subjects in a composition of three to five paragraphs.

1. In "The First Snow-Fall," the snow clearly held a meaning for the speaker that went beyond the heaps of whiteness he saw covering the earth. Lowell refers to snow as the "noiseless work of the sky," the "patience/ That fell...like snow," and "the snow that husheth all." A *symbol* is something that stands for something beyond itself. What does the snow represent, and what good does it bring to someone who sorrows?

2. Which of the poems you have read thus far in this chapter has the most universality, is the best expression of feelings most people share at one time or another? Of course, you can only judge for yourself. This means there can be no right or wrong answer.

    Why do you feel that it is easier to see through the eyes of one speaker than another? Explain the reasons for your choice, being sure you have good examples on which to base your opinion.

Literal, Figurative, or Both?

When you take words literally, you take them at face value as meaning exactly what they say.

In "The First Snow-Fall," what did Lowell mean by writing that snow fell all night long? Of course, just that! It's a silly question, but the kind that gets asked when people tie themselves up in knots about poetry. But how can you tell when a poet is using a word literally? Here are three rules that should help.

> *Rule One:* If a statement makes literal sense, first take it literally. Always accept words at their face value, if you can.

Lowell also stated that the trees were wearing ermine. A pine tree draped in fur? That can't be! So it must be taken figuratively, as a metaphor that emphasizes the softness, beauty, and richness of the snow.

> *Rule Two:* If a word doesn't fit literally, try picturing it as a metaphor, or comparison.

But what about the snow? Wasn't it also a symbol?

Yes, sometimes you can have it both ways—literally and figuratively—as in "The First Snow-Fall."

Rule Three: To understand the meaning of a symbol, follow these three steps.

1. Know how the symbol was used literally in the poem.

> EXAMPLE: In "The First Snow-Fall," the snow had fallen at night, covering and softening the harshness of the earth. The speaker also thought of its covering the mound of his young daughter's grave.

2. Know what the symbol stands for.

> EXAMPLE: The snow stands for the healing gift of patience that comes to ease the man's sorrow.

3. Know how the symbol makes it easier to understand the thing it stands for.

> EXAMPLE: Just as the snow fell silently from the sky to renew the earth with its soft whiteness, so does the quiet work of God bring comforting acceptance to ease the speaker's sorrow.

Other poems may be less direct, so always be prepared to follow the clues the poet gives you.

An Extra Dimension

Before you begin reading the following poem, think of the picture that is brought to mind by the words *southern mansion*. Describe some of the things you see. What is your image of the people living there?

Instead of expressing their ideas in general terms, poets like to use a specific person, place, or incident to represent an entire group. By concentrating on an individual example, the poet puts you in closer contact with the subject and makes it easier for you to share her or his vision. In this case, one southern mansion stands as a symbol for all, and the entire poem represents a past way of life.

Although the following poem is titled "Southern Mansion," Bontemps uses few details to describe the mansion itself. As you read, discover how Bontemps's poem compares with your stereotyped or preconceived notion, and decide why he chose to omit more specific details.

Southern Mansion

Poplars are standing there still as death
And ghosts of dead men
Meet their ladies walking
Two by two beneath the shade
And standing on the marble steps.   5

There is a sound of music echoing
Through the open door
And in the field there is
Another sound tinkling in the cotton:
Chains of bondmen* dragging on the ground.   10

The years go back with an iron clank,
A hand is on the gate,
A dry leaf trembles on the wall.
Ghosts are walking.
They have broken roses down   15
And poplars stand there still as death.

——Arna Bontemps

10. **bondmen:** people in bondage; slaves.

FOCUSING IN

Write your answers on a separate piece of paper.

1. Haunting the mansion are ghosts
   a. from the American Revolution
   b. from before the Civil War
   c. from the Great Depression
   d. from the postwar carpetbagger era.

2. The ghosts in the first stanza represent
   a. members of plantation-owning families
   b. all who lived in the South
   c. the owners of the mansion
   d. Southern governors and politicians.

3. The words *two by two* and *music* are used to create the impression of what kind of occasion?

4. In the first stanza, what one word symbolizes the luxury of the mansion itself?

5. What phrase in stanza 2 directly echoes ''sound of music''? What do the ''chains of bondmen'' symbolize?

6. ''An iron clank'' suggests the
   a. bombardment during the war
   b. locking of the mansion door
   c. sound of chains
   d. hopelessness of the Southern cause.

7. In stanza 3, the ''hand...on the gate'' and the ghosts belong to
   a. soldiers
   b. spies
   c. slaves
   d. all humanity.

8. Line 15, ''They have broken roses down,'' adds to the idea that these ghosts are
   a. heading to the mansion
   b. running away
   c. part of the invading army
   d. eager to join the party and have fun.

9. The poplars of lines 1 and 16 are seen to be
   a. lovely guardians of a glorious past
   b. indifferent and superior to men
   c. warnings of death and evil to come
   d. silent onlookers to lives of ease and wealth founded on injustice.

10. What elements in this poem differ from the traditional description of a southern mansion?

Will You Agree?

To understand the following poem, ''The Bare Tree,'' you must be prepared to read the poem's words on several levels. On the first, the speaker asks you to take his words literally and agree that his conclusion is the right one.

Second, comes the logical level. Decide whether the poet, William Carlos Williams, wants you to agree with the speaker's opinion, using logic to support your stand.

Be sure of the poem's literal and logical senses before trying to reach the third level, the figurative meaning. You can't know how the bare tree serves as a symbol without first understanding the poet's intent.

The Bare Tree

The bare cherry tree
higher than the roof
last year produced
abundant fruit. But how
speak of fruit confronted   5
by that skeleton?
Though live it may be
there is no fruit on it.
Therefore chop it down
and use the wood   10
against this biting cold.

——William Carlos Williams

THINKING IT THROUGH

1. On a literal level:
   Give two facts about the bare tree.
   What proves whether the tree is still alive?
   What time of year is it?
   What does the speaker plan to do with the wood?

2. On a logical level:
   Why does the speaker feel that the tree deserves to be chopped down?
   Why are there no cherries on the tree?
   Why does the speaker want the tree thought of as a skeleton?
   Is or isn't the tree a skeleton literally?

3. On a figurative level: Something seems missing from the poem. If you aren't expected to agree with the speaker, Williams must intend the bare tree to have a symbolic meaning.
   People concern themselves with the present, past, and future. Which concerns the speaker of this poem?
   Which one interests him most?
   What does he apparently fail to realize?
   Which of the following might the tree symbolize—a person's blindness to future needs; people who live only for today; the unthinking destruction of nature; appearances that are misleading? Choose one of these closely related ideas or one of your own, and explain the symbolism in ''The Bare Tree,'' including how the symbol is used literally, what it stands for, and how it makes the underlying idea easier to understand.

On Your Own

What does Stephen Crane mean by the "ball of gold"? Enter your ideas and questions in your notebook.

A man saw a ball of gold

A man saw a ball of gold in the sky;
He climbed for it,
And eventually he achieved it—
It was clay.

Now this is the strange part.   5
When the man went to the earth
And looked again,
Lo, there was the ball of gold.

Now is the strange part:
It was a ball of gold.   10
Aye, by the heavens, it was a ball of gold.

——Stephen Crane

Refining and Expanding

Skillful writing often requires you to choose between two opposite techniques, both important to good editing.

Refining: Sometimes writing needs to be polished or pruned to eliminate unnecessary words that distract from your idea. It's similar to the refining process for oil, metals, and sugar—removing what does not belong from the final product.

Compare the following examples.

Unrefined: The game was for the championship, and our team won it with a basket at the last minute. It was exciting.

Refined: Our team won the championship game with an exciting last-minute basket.

The second version takes only twelve words to say what the first does in twenty-one. How would you refine the following? Remember, there is no one right way, only the goal of making it clearer and more concise.

> There was a note of doubt in her voice as she spoke of her chances of winning the election for president of the sophomore class.

Expanding: At times, an idea needs fuller development and more detail to make it easier to grasp. Expanding is also a useful technique when you are trying to get at the meaning of some lines of poetry. For example, take this line by Alexander Pope:

> To err is human; to forgive, divine.

In an expanded version, it might read as follows:

> Human beings, because they are human, make mistakes, but when a person forgives someone else, it shows a goodness that deserves comparison to godliness.

EXPERIMENTING WITH WORDS AND IDEAS

Everyone likes to think that his or her favorite is the greatest . . . number one . . . at the head of the list. Every year advertisers spend millions trying to convince you that their product is the best. Poll takers survey voters, as if popularity counted more than political beliefs.

Is being best-liked the same as being the best?

Take a survey in your class to see how much agreement you find.

On your own paper or on a ballot, list your choice of "The Best" for each of the following categories. No peeking until all decisions are made, or you'll spoil the validity of the poll.

1. Professional football team

2. Professional basketball player

3. Musical group

4. Individual singer

5. Movie you've seen this year

6. Situation comedy on television

7. Make of automobile

8. Soft drink or soda

9. Place in the world for a vacation

10. Book you've ever read

After tallying your survey, how many clear-cut bests did your class come up with? Is it really possible to name one of anything as the absolute best? Why or why not?

Elizabeth Barrett Browning uses highly refined language as she explains her selection of "The Best." In a first reading, identify her choices and decide what you think of her list.

The Best

What's the best thing in the world?
June-roses, by May-dew impearl'd;
Sweet south-wind, that means no rain;
Truth, not cruel to a friend;
Pleasure, not in haste to end;   5
Beauty, not self-deck'd* and curl'd
Till its pride is over-plain;
Light, that never makes you wink;
Memory, that gives no pain;
Love, when, so, you're loved again.   10
What's the best thing in the world?
—Something out of it, I think.

————Elizabeth Barrett Browning

6. **self-deck'd:** self-decorated.

THINKING IT THROUGH

1. What eight items does Browning nominate as her choices for the "best thing in the world"? Which are concrete and which abstract?

2. Browning has written compressed statements about her choices. For example, line 4 states, "Truth, not cruel to a friend." An expanded version might read, "The best thing in the world is truth, so long as revealing it would not hurt someone close to you." Write expanded versions of Browning's other choices, being careful to maintain her intended meaning.

3. Which of the choices that name concrete things may also serve as symbols and represent abstract qualities? Explain what they stand for and why.

4. What does Browning mean by saying that the best thing in the world is "something out of it"?

5. How does this express a typically human attitude or feeling?

The Importance of the Unsaid

Robert Frost is one of America's best-known, most-liked poets. One reason for his popularity is the naturalness with which he voices feelings that many people share.

But read carefully. There are ideas lurking beneath the surface that may escape the unthoughtful reader. As you read this poem on its literal level, be alert for the basic comparison the speaker makes. The right conclusions prepare you for sharing the poem's deeper, figurative sense.

The Road Not Taken

Two roads diverged* in a yellow wood,
And sorry I could not travel both
And be one traveler, long I stood
And looked down one as far as I could
To where it bent in the undergrowth;   5

Then took the other, as just as fair,
And having perhaps the better claim
Because it was grassy and wanted* wear;
Though as for that the passing there
Had worn them really about the same.   10

And both that morning equally lay
In leaves no step had trodden black.
Oh, I kept the first for another day!
Yet knowing how way leads on to way,
I doubted if I should ever come back.   15

I shall be telling this with a sigh
Somewhere ages and ages hence:*
Two roads diverged in a wood, and I—
I took the one less traveled by,
And that has made all the difference.   20

——Robert Frost

---

1. diverged: branched off in different directions. **8. wanted:** lacked. **17. hence:** in the future.

FOCUSING IN

1. The speaker tells of a choice
   a. made in the past
   b. to be made in the future
   c. made when suffering a great loss
   d. after becoming lost in the woods.

2. The words *travel* and *traveler* indicate the speaker was most likely
   a. out for an autumn hike
   b. going on some kind of journey
   c. conducting an exploration
   d. following a map.

3. In stanza 1 the speaker tells of
   a. being at a crossroad
   b. standing at the branch of two roads
   c. looking back where the road stretched behind him
   d. having to push through dense undergrowth.

4. The speaker would have preferred to
   a. have someone else along
   b. be another traveler
   c. travel both roads
   d. go part way down one before making the choice.

5. Write the three words that show the speaker took time in making the decision.

6. From lines 6–11, list three phrases that prove the roads were practically equal.

7. The speaker expresses doubt about the
   a. direction that was taken
   b. difficulties that lay ahead
   c. fact that no one else had trod on the leaves
   d. chances of returning to the spot.

8. Write the phrase in stanza 4 that is an obvious exaggeration.

9. The speaker uses this exaggeration
   a. to add a note of humor
   b. as an ironical comment on the situation
   c. to point up bitterness
   d. to emphasize the importance of the choice.

10. By "telling this with a sigh," the speaker shows regret for
    a. not being able to take both roads
    b. having made the wrong decision
    c. having wasted time at the crossroads
    d. being so thoroughly misunderstood.

THINKING IT THROUGH

It's clear the choice made in "The Road Not Taken" affected the speaker deeply. Why does the speaker consider these roads so important? What does the road he took symbolize? Your answers to the following questions will lead to an understanding of the poem's figurative meaning. Remember, don't think of the speaker as being a poet. The incident could be from almost anyone's life—maybe yours.

1. It is only in the next-to-last line that the speaker describes the road taken as "the one less traveled by." Earlier in the poem, what conclusion is made after a comparison between the two roads?

2. Why did Frost call this poem "The Road Not Taken"? What would be the difference if he had titled it "The Road Less Traveled"?

3. Considering the title, which really is the more important of the two roads? Why is the one he didn't take so important to the speaker?

4. Why might the speaker feel exactly the same way after making the opposite choice?

5. With this in mind, how would changing the title to "The Road Less Traveled" show that the speaker was trying to prove his choice was right?

6. What made all the difference?

7. Why is the speaker so interested in "the road not taken?" What lines throughout the poem support your conclusion?

8. How is "the road not taken" a symbol? How does it bring to clear view a situation that anyone may face in life?

Expressing Your Ideas

From "The First Snow-Fall" to "The Road Not Taken," several of the poems in this chapter are about an incident in a person's life. Although these incidents do not seem momentous, they are the kind that shape everyone's life. And they awaken feelings that everyone can share.

Do the poets simply tell what happened? No, that wouldn't be enough. The purpose is to bring the incident into sharp focus, to give it dimension and meaning. In order to trace thoughts to their conclusion, a writer may add or take away details, expand or refine. He or she may even adopt a new persona.

Is there an incident in your life that seemed insignificant but that later came to influence how you think and who you are?

Write a few paragraphs or a poem describing such an incident in clear, precise words. Try to refine your writing so that every word counts, yet include details that allow your reader to share in your experience.

As you write, try to see the event in your imagination so you can capture it accurately on paper. Be sure to direct your reader toward the understanding you gained.

You might also want to try out how it feels to be in someone else's skin. Pick a moment in someone else's life—someone very different from you—and describe what it would be like to look through his or her eyes. For example, what would it be like to be a new student just entering your school? Or a new teacher?

Summing Up

Word for word, poetry carries more meaning than other forms of writing. Poets refine their writing so that it holds more than surface meaning.

Well-written poetry invites you to plunge in, and the more your eyes are opened to its depths, the more you'll see within. That's why a really good poem is never boring. There's always something new to discover inside.

In order to draw reasonable conclusions about a poem, you need to know where the poet is "coming from." Be on the lookout for important clues that help you become more expert at understanding and making judgments about the poems you read.

C H A P T E R   S I X

Composition: Bringing It All Together

ave you ever felt a touch of stage fright? And then someone said, "Compose yourself," meaning pull yourself together and present a calm, self-assured appearance to the world.

As well as composing yourself, you can also compose a letter or a song, a photograph or a painting, a newspaper story or—of course—a poem.

Composition is the act of "putting together." It means bringing separate elements together so that each contributes smoothly to the total effect of the whole.

When you become aware of the groundwork laid through composition, you gain a deeper understanding of what you see, hear, and read.

In planning a painting, artists compose their pictures so your eyes will stay inside the frame and not stray away from the subject. Through careful composition, an artist also directs your gaze to move easily around the picture and not become stuck in one place.

Compare the three diagrams below to see how this happens.

Which diagram points you out of the picture? Which draws you to a stop and leaves you there? Which directs your attention back and forth for a fuller look?

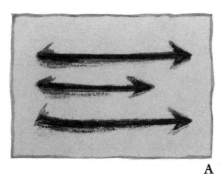

A   B   C

In many ways, the composition of a picture and of a poem are similar. A good poem invites you to "stay inside," directs you through its ideas, and uses its details to help guide your understanding.

Take another look at "Southern Mansion" on page 88. Arna Bontemps begins his poem "Poplars are standing there still as death" and ends with almost the same words. These two lines serve as a frame, asking you to notice how the entire poem fits together inside. When you compare the two sets of "ghosts...walking," you discover the secret that the Southern Mansion tried to keep hidden from the world—that, perhaps, the "men [and] their ladies" kept hidden from themselves.

Seeing the End in the Beginning

At first glance, Emily Dickinson's short poem seems childishly simple. A closer look reveals the great care she must have taken in composing it.

An important technique in composition is *parallel construction*.

EXAMPLE:
I saw him; he saw me.
Ann wanted to go; Lynn decided to stay.

Poets often use parallel lines as an invitation to make comparisons. Ask yourself how the lines are alike. How and why are they different? And, after becoming aware of patterns, be alert for changes—they're sure to be important.

I never saw a moor

I never saw a moor,*
I never saw the sea
Yet know I how the heather* looks,
And what a wave must be.

I never spoke with God,   5
Nor visited in heaven,
Yet certain am I of the spot
As if the chart* were given.

——Emily Dickinson

1. **moor:** an open space of land often covered with heather. 3. **heather:** shrubs with pinkish-purple flowers that grow extensively in Scotland and England and are frequently referred to in novels and poems about those countries. 8. **chart:** a map.

T H I N K I N G   I T   T H R O U G H

1. What three lines in Dickinson's poem are parallel or nearly so?

2. In the first stanza what would make the speaker so confident of knowing about two things that she has never seen? Give three possible sources for gaining this knowledge. Do you think those sources provide sufficient information for knowing without actually seeing?

3. In line 5 the speaker says "I never spoke with God." Because of the parallel composition, what idea follows that need not be said?

4. Based on the reasoning behind stanza 1, explain why the speaker feels able to express such certainty about heaven in stanza 2.

5. Dickinson could have composed the first stanza of her poem like the one following. How would it have changed the way that you move through the poem? What changes would it make in the attitude that the speaker expresses?

> I know how the heather looks,
>   Yet never saw a moor;
> I know what a wave must be,
>   Yet haven't seen a shore.

6. How would the rewritten version affect the second stanza? In both versions, what conclusion are you expected to draw from the examples given?

Choosing the Better Way

Form also involves the interrelations among the ideas and images in a poem, and parallel construction makes these relationships easier to discern. Did Emily Dickinson just happen upon a moor and the sea as images paralleling heaven, or did she have good reasons for her choices? What would the poem be like with a different set of examples? Compare the version on page 102 with the original, and decide why Emily Dickinson's images more closely fit the concept of heaven.

I never saw an alp

I never saw an alp
  I never saw a dune;
Yet know I how a mountain looks,
  And how the sand must loom.

I never spoke with God,   5
  Nor visited in heaven;
Yet certain am I of the spot
  As if the chart were given.

——Annalee Pinkerton

THINKING IT THROUGH

1. What is wrong with comparing an alp to heaven? What does it make you see that does not fit?

2. How does the physical sensation usually associated with an alp also spoil this comparison?

3. Why doesn't a dune serve as a good comparison to heaven? How does it create a feeling opposite from the one expressed by *alp,* but also ineffective?

4. In what ways do *moor* and *sea* create images that are parallel and similar to images associated with heaven?

5. How would the effect change if the last stanza were fully parallel to the first?

> I never spoke with God,
>   Nor went to heaven above;
> Yet certain am I God exists
>   And rules the sky with love.

Does it improve or worsen the composition of the poem? Explain.

Form Determines Meaning: A Dialogue

"Nothing is real except the mist, and the mist is not real either."
"What's that?"
"It's just a thought."
"Is it a poem?"
"It's in my head like a poem. Only I don't know how to put it on paper so it will look and sound the way I see and hear it in my mind."

Nothing is real
except the mist
and the mist is
not real either.

"You like that better?"
"Not much. It's too solid. It looks the opposite of what it's trying to say."

Nothing
is
real except
the mist
and
the mist
is
not real either.

"Is that the real poem?"
"It's only real when I decide it's written to be read as closely as possible to my understanding of it."

Nothing is real
   except
      the mist
(and
   the mist) is
not real
   either

Experimenting with Form

In poetry, form concerns itself with the organization and placement of each of the elements. Form may be strictly predetermined, like a sonnet, into which words are poured—so many syllables to a line, so many lines, so many rhymes.

The form can also be free verse, with no fixed pattern, rhyme, or rhythm. Yet even free verse doesn't just happen. Because there's no formal scheme to guide the reader, the writer of free verse has extra responsibility to make every detail meaningful.

In the dialogue about form, you saw three poetic versions of the same words. Each emphasizes specific words that might be lost or skipped over if written in prose.

In a paragraph, the greatest attention generally goes to the first and the last sentences. In a sentence, concentration falls on the first word and the last.

Poetry puts an extra emphasis on the first and last words of every line. And, in free verse, a poet can spotlight a word by setting it off on a line all by itself.

Reread the three versions of "Nothing." Notice how each asks you to concentrate on different words, to pause, or to increase your tempo of reading, simply by changing the form.

These same twelve words could take many other forms, each carrying different meanings and asking to be read differently. After experimenting with versions of your own, choose two you like best and share them with your class.

A Tall Tale in Free Verse

Just by looking at it, you can tell the following poem is written in free verse. It's just about as free as you can get! In "nobody loses all the time," E. E. Cummings breaks the rules of normal punctuation—and a number of other rules, too. How many "mistakes" in punctuation and capitalization can you find?

That doesn't mean this poem lacks thought and organization. In many ways, it's like a tall tale, and so the truth must be stretched a little more with each new development. Note how the poem is divided into episodes, and watch for unusual breaks at the ends of lines and between stanzas. Be prepared to discover why so much freedom of form is the perfect complement to Uncle Sol's life story.

nobody loses all the time

nobody loses all the time

i had an uncle named
Sol who was a born failure and
nearly everybody said he should have gone
into vaudeville perhaps because my Uncle Sol could   5
sing McCann He Was A Diver on Xmas Eve like Hell Itself* which
may or may not account for the fact that my Uncle

Sol indulged in that possibly most inexcusable
of all to use a highfalooting* phrase
luxuries that is or to   10
wit* farming and be
it needlessly
added

my Uncle Sol's farm
failed because the chickens   15
ate the vegetables so
my Uncle Sol had a
chicken farm till the
skunks ate the chickens when

my Uncle Sol   20
had a skunk farm but
the skunks caught cold and
died and so
my Uncle Sol imitated the
skunks in a subtle manner   25

or by drowning himself in the watertank
but somebody who'd given my Uncle Sol a Victor
Victrola and records while he lived presented to
him upon the auspicious* occasion of his decease a
scrumptious not to mention splendiferous funeral with   30
tall boys in black gloves and flowers and everything and

i remember we all cried like the Missouri
when my Uncle Sol's coffin lurched because
somebody pressed a button
(and down went   35
my Uncle Sol

and started a worm farm)

                                                    ——E. E. Cummings

6. like Hell Itself: loud and rowdy. 9. highfalooting: attempting to impress as
high class. 11. to wit: that is to say, namely. 29. auspicious: promising, full of
favorable prospects.

THINKING IT THROUGH

Once in a while almost everyone has a taste for humor that's deliciously dark and offbeat, else why would so many people laugh during horror movies? Maybe there's cheer in the thought that things are never so bad that they can't get worse—so you can consider yourself lucky no matter what befalls. After all, nobody loses all the time. Does Uncle Sol prove this or not? Reserve judgment until you've answered the following questions.

1. Two of the first clues about the unusual notions in Cummings' poem are the unconventionality of its form and the fact there's not a period to be found. To see the change of effect, rewrite the poem in sentences with standard punctuation and capitalization. Here's how lines 1–10 might go:

   > Nobody loses all the time. I had an uncle named Sol who was a born failure. Nearly everyone said he should have gone into vaudeville. Perhaps this was because my Uncle Sol could sing "McCann, He Was a Diver" on Christmas Eve as loud as the devil. This may or may not account for the fact that my Uncle Sol participated in that most inexcusable of all (to use a fancy phrase) luxuries—namely, farming.

   In groups of four, work out a version of the following sets of lines: 11–19, 20–26, 27–31, and 32–37. Compare your version with the original. How does it read? What effect did Cummings create through form and unusual usage?

2. What "highfalooting" phrases does the speaker use? What contrasts tell you the speaker was just trying to "put on airs"? Does Cummings lead you to take the speaker's judgments seriously? Why or why not?

3. What reasons might there be for saying that running a farm is a "most inexcusable luxury"? What problems might a farmer encounter that makes farming a constant gamble?

4. Like a tall tale, the story gets wilder with every new step. From lines 11–23, what three steps tell the tale of Uncle Sol's farming attempts? What seems utterly unbelievable and why?

5. In lines 24–26 what comparison does Cummings make? How does he make it impossible to feel sorry for Uncle Sol?

6. Do lines 27–31 show Uncle Sol living up (or dying down) to the promise of the first line? Why or why not?

7. How and why is the last line of the poem a surprise? At the same time, how has Cummings prepared so that the line doesn't seem cruel or out of place?

8. Does Uncle Sol serve as a good example of the slogan "Nobody loses all the time"?

9. Why might being able to laugh at Sol's impossible bad luck not be so bad after all?

EXPERIMENTING WITH WORDS AND IDEAS

Discover how much you can change an idea just by changing its form. Begin with a thought of your own or a found quotation that especially interests you.

In deciding on your arrangement of words, you can find inspiration in poems you've read or develop a form of your own. You can vary line length, punctuation, capitalization. You can repeat words or omit words, space them out or break them apart.

Remember, like tone of voice, emphasis, and pauses, the form you choose should be a guide to clearer understanding.

As an example, let's begin with a found quotation:

8:30 WILD AMERICA
    More than just a fur coat, the mink is also as graceful as an otter, feisty as a wolverine, and pungent under stress as a skunk.
    —From *TV 30.FM 91 Guide,* June 1990

Wild America

More than
just
$$$ a fur coat $$$
a mink
is also as graceful as
an otter
feisty as a wolverine
and
pungent under stress as
a skunk

An Unfashionable Tale

More than just?
a fur
coattheMINK is also
as graceful
        as an otter
as feisty
        as a wolverine
and, pungent
(under stress)
        as a skunk.

Choose your idea in one of these ways:

1. Pick a sentence or two from a newspaper, a magazine, a book, a set of directions, an encyclopedia, and so forth. Seek words that might have an entirely new dimension if given a new form. Be sure you know the source (title, author if given, and page number).

2. Write a statement of your own, something you've thought about but never put in words before. You might begin "I wonder why . . ." or "If only . . ." to start you thinking.

On your paper, write the item as a standard sentence or paragraph, and include two favorite versions in poetic form.

Comparing Traditional and Free Verse

At first glance, the following poems seem more similar than different. Both are short, both concern kings, both have a similar form—and both show how poets take advantage of form to emphasize ideas. One poem was written in traditional form in the seventeenth century and the other in free verse in the twentieth. Notice how form determines the placement of key words, and compare the attitudes each poet expresses toward a similar subject.

Lion

The lion is called the king
Of beasts. Nowadays there are
Almost as many lions
In cages as out of them.
If offered a crown, refuse.

——Kenneth Rexroth

Epitaph on Charles II

Here lies our Sovereign Lord the King,
Whose word no man relies on,
Who never said a foolish thing,
Nor ever did a wise one.

————John Wilmot, Earl of Rochester

Epitaph: a brief statement in memory of a deceased person. **Charles II:** (1630–1685) king of England, 1660–1685.

THINKING IT THROUGH

1. How do the first lines of each poem show how the placement of a key word gives it emphasis?

2. Which of the two poems is written with more naturally grouped words and phrases on the same line? Which is free verse?

3. How does Rexroth's poem lead you to see unexpected relationships between certain words and phrases?

4. How does Rexroth use form to bring out the poem's irony?

5. In the terms of the poem, why should you refuse a crown if you are offered one?

6. Since openings for real-life kings are rare nowadays, what might the lion in this poem symbolize?

7. In "Epitaph," how does the rhyming of the second and fourth lines call attention to the reason that "no man relies on" the king's word? Although he "never said a foolish thing," why did no one trust him?

8. The first two words call attention to the poem's being an epitaph. Given the rest of the poem, what might be the pun in the words "Here lies..."?

9. What makes the "Epitaph on Charles II" ironical?

10. Why is (or isn't) the form chosen for each of these poems effective? Why does Wilmot's poem have universality?

Repetition and Variation

Because of form, one repeated word pops out of the following poem. Can you imagine yourself sitting in a lecture room thinking, "When...when...when ...when"? What would you be asking yourself? The poem is free verse, yes, but a closer analysis shows how much form contributes to your understanding of the speaker's feeling.

Compare the lengths of the first four lines and see how their pattern of composition adds to the effect. The poem divides into two parts. Try to determine the purpose for this division. How does form help you appreciate the difference between the lecturer's attitude toward the stars and the listener's?

When I Heard the Learn'd Astronomer

When I heard the learn'd astronomer,
When the proofs, the figures, were ranged in columns before me,
When I was shown the charts and diagrams, to add, divide, and
    measure them,
When I sitting heard the astronomer where he lectured with much
    applause in the lecture room,
How soon unaccountable I became sick and tired,   5

Till rising and gliding out I wandered off by myself,
In the mystical moist night air, and from time to time,
Looked up in perfect silence at the stars.

——Walt Whitman

THINKING IT THROUGH

1. What is the setting and situation in the first four lines? What proves this isn't a college class?

2. What idea did the poet convey by using the word *lectured* instead of *spoke* in line 4? Do such words as *columns, charts, diagrams,* and *measure* make the lecture seem lively and exciting or formal and dull? Why do they have this effect?

3. The word *heard* is used twice in the first four lines. How does this word differ in effect from *listened?*

4. How do the repetition and parallel structure in lines 1–4 express the attitude of the person leaving the lecture?

5. In line 5, the speaker says, "How soon unaccountable I became sick and tired." Why is the word *unaccountable* ironic? What actually accounts for his reaction?

6. Compare the verb forms *were ranged* and *was shown* in lines 1–4 with *rising, gliding,* and *wandered* in line 6. What difference in effect do they have?

7. How does calling the night air "mystical" contrast the speaker's attitude with the astronomer's?

8. How does the word *learn'd* have a sense similar to *were ranged* and *was shown?* Taking the entire poem into consideration, how does the word *learn'd* have both a literal and an ironic sense?

9. What is the significance of the last line of the poem? How do the words *perfect* and *silence* contrast with the presentation of astronomy in the first four lines?

Fixing on Form

Like a chair or an airplane, a poem is usually easy to identify. But that's far from saying all poems are alike. Every time a poet writes, he or she must choose or invent a form, one that will best express the idea that's taking shape in the poet's mind.

A poem can be any length, from a pair of lines to a book-length narrative.

A poem can be complete in a couplet (two equal lines that usually rhyme), as this poem by William Blake shows:

> Great things are done when Men & Mountains meet
> This is not done by Jostling in the Street.

Poets sometimes write in quatrains (groups of four lines), as James Russell Lowell did in these selected stanzas from ''The First Snow-Fall'':

> The snow had begun in the gloaming,
>   And busily all the night
> Had been heaping field and highway
>   With a silence deep and white.
>
> Every pine and fir and hemlock
>   Wore ermine too dear for an earl,
> And the poorest twig on the elm-tree
>   Was ridged inch deep with pearl.
>
> From sheds new-roofed with Carrara
>   Came Chanticleer's muffled crow,
> The stiff rails softened to swan's-down,
>   And still fluttered down the snow.
>
> I stood and watched by the window
>   The noiseless work of the sky,
> And the sudden flurries of snow-birds,
>   Like brown leaves whirling by.

Of course, stanzas can have any number of lines. . .and, if that doesn't inspire you, there's always free verse. The choices are almost endless!

Dana Gioia writes of this aspect of poetry in ''The Next Poem.''

The Next Poem

How much better it seems now
than when it is finally done—
the unforgettable first line,
the cunning way the stanzas run.

The rhymes (for, yes, it will have rhymes)   5
almost inaudible at first,
an appetite not yet acknowledged
like the inkling of a thirst.

While gradually the form appears
as each line is coaxed aloud—   10
the architecture of a room
seen from the middle of a crowd.

The music that of common speech
but slanted so that each detail
sounds unexpected as a sharp*   15
inserted in a simple scale.

No jumble box of imagery
dumped glumly in the reader's lap
or elegantly packaged junk
the unsuspecting must unwrap.   20

But words that could direct a friend
precisely to an unknown place,
those few unshakeable details
no confusion can erase.

And the real subject left unspoken   25
but unmistakeable to those
who don't expect a jungle parrot
in the black and white of prose.

How much better it seems now
than when it is finally written.   30
How hungrily one waits to feel
the bright lure* seized, the old hook bitten.

——Dana Gioia

---

15. sharp: a musical note one-half step higher than a natural. **32. lure:** artificial
bait used to catch fish.

FOCUSING IN

Write your answers on a separate piece of paper.

1. "The Next Poem" is written in
   a. couplets
   b. unrhymed quatrains
   c. rhymed quatrains
   d. free verse.

2. From the use of capitalization, punctuation, and vocabulary, the poet most likely
   a. lived before the twentieth century
   b. lived in the twentieth century
   c. is inexperienced with form
   d. is ignorant of grammar.

3. In the first stanza, "it" is
   a. an entire poem not yet written
   b. "the unforgettable first line"
   c. a metaphor for the poetic impulse
   d. "the cunning way the stanzas run."

4. In stanza 2, "an appetite not yet acknowledged" is
   a. a simile for the thirst for understanding
   b. an ironic reference to the supposed ease of writing poetry
   c. a symbol of the poet's hunger to be published
   d. a metaphor for the poem's need to rhyme.

5. Comparing form to architecture, stanza 3 implies that form
   a. is chiefly decoration
   b. should be the poet's main concern
   c. is better appreciated read aloud
   d. is difficult to maintain while choosing from a "crowd" of words.

6. Because stanza 4 deals with the sound of poetry, the words "simple scale" in line 16 must refer to
   a. a musical scale
   b. the importance of weighing every word
   c. the iridescence of words, like pearly scales of fish
   d. the height of poetry, as in scaling a mountain.

7. In stanzas 5 and 6, the speaker criticizes
   a. fussy and too precise attention to details
   b. the confusing and misleading use of metaphors and symbols
   c. critics who compare poetry to a jumble box
   d. the idea of words being like friends.

8. Line 25 leads one to conclude that the real subject of this poem is
   a. the next poem
   b. the clarity of prose
   c. left unspoken
   d. how poetry is colorful, like a parrot.

9. By comparing writing a poem to catching a fish on a baited hook, the speaker implies that the final outcome is
   a. a great catch
   b. an unforgettable experience
   c. a cunning trick
   d. a painful disappointment.

10. The entire poem can stand as a symbol of how
    a. it's a waste of time to try too hard
    b. you should not trust your first impulses
    c. judging by appearances leads to error
    d. things often seem better in the imagination than in reality.

On Your Own

Write your impression of this Sylvia Plath poem. Include a comparison between it and "The Next Poem" on page 113.

Stillborn

These poems do not live: it's a sad diagnosis.
They grew their toes and fingers well enough,
Their little foreheads bulged with concentration.
If they missed out on walking about like people
It wasn't for any lack of mother love.   5

O I cannot understand what happened to them!
They are proper in shape and number and every part.
They sit so nicely in the pickling fluid!
They smile and smile and smile and smile at me.
And still the lungs won't fill and the heart won't start.   10

They are not pigs, they are not even fish,
Though they have a piggy and a fishy air—
It would be better if they were alive, and that's what they were.
But they are dead, and their mother near dead with distraction,
And they stupidly stare, and do not speak of her.

——Sylvia Plath

Two Poems?

Read the following selection. Clearly, the speaker is deeply upset by something—"What is it that to fury I am roused?"—and is trying to reason with himself—"what moment is it. . .?" Briefly sum up the idea that the speaker expresses toward life and the world.

When I gaze at the sun
and know that this great earth
is but a fragment thrown
in heat and flame a billion years ago,
that then this world was lifeless
as, a billion hence,
it shall again be,
what moment* is it that I am betrayed,
oppressed, cast down,
or warm with love or triumph?

What is it that to fury I am roused?
What meaning for me
in this homeless clan
the dupe of space
the toy of time

Now read the following. In contrast to the previous selection, this selection focuses on a specific incident and tells the story of a hateful encounter. Decide why the speaker says "still it takes a moment."

I walked to the subway booth
for change for a dime.
Two adolescent girls stood there
alive with eagerness to know
all in their new found world
there was for them to know
they looked at me and brightly asked
"Are you Arabian?"
I smiled and cautiously
—for one grows cautious—
shook my head.
"Egyptian?"
Again I smiled and shook my head
and walked away.
I've gone but seven paces now
and from behind comes swift the sneer
"Or Nigger?"

A moment, please
for still it takes a moment
and now
I'll turn
and smile
and nod my head.

Compare the two selections, and decide what is the subject of each.

Which poem seems the easier to understand? Which one seems to take a broader and more thoughtful look at existence?

In reality, this is one poem, not two. When you read "A Moment Please," the following poem, in its original version, you will discover a new dimension—totally a result of form.

If you met the poem for the first time without knowing the secret of its form, you might find its essential ideas difficult to extract. Understanding its form makes all the difference, and "A Moment Please" illustrates how form affects meaning.

A Moment Please

When I gaze at the sun
  I walked to the subway booth
  for change for a dime.
and know that this great earth
  Two adolescent girls stood there   5
  alive with eagerness to know
is but a fragment thrown
  all in their new found world
  there was for them to know
in heat and flame a billion years ago,   10
  they looked at me and brightly asked
  "Are you Arabian?"
that then this world was lifeless
  I smiled and cautiously
  —for one grows cautious—   15
  shook my head.
as, a billion hence,
  "Egyptian?"
it shall again be,
  Again I smiled and shook my head   20
  and walked away.
what moment* is it that I am betrayed,
  I've gone but seven paces now
oppressed, cast down,
  and from behind comes swift the sneer 25
or warm with love or triumph?
  "Or Nigger?"

  A moment, please
What is it that to fury I am roused?
  for still it takes a moment   30
What meaning for me
  and now
in this homeless clan
  I'll turn
the dupe of space   35
  and smile
the toy of time
  and nod my head.

—Samuel Allen (Paul Vesey)

22. **what moment:** of what importance.

THINKING IT THROUGH

1. When the incident at the subway booth is printed alone, what is the speaker's outward reaction to the girls' sneering question?

2. What must the girls have thought about his response?

3. How does the complete poem reveal his real feelings about the treatment he received?

4. What do the speaker's thoughts show about a person's ability to shrug off insults of this kind?

5. What words in the poem refer to time?

6. What two different meanings of the word *moment* does the poet use in lines 22, 28, and 30?

7. In what ways is the speaker "the toy of time"?

8. This poem is based on a racial slur. In what ways does everyone have similar situations in his or her life?

Summing Up

An essential difference between poetry and other kinds of writing is form.

Through skillful composition, the parts of a poem fit together as a whole, yet provide a framework that directs your attention to important details that hold the poem's meaning. Poetic form involves countless choices about how a poem is organized. Is it free verse or composed of rhymed stanzas? What pattern is common to its images? How do parallel lines and repetition help you smoothly follow the poet's train of thought?

All the elements of form (rhythm, order, the interrelation of words and images) work together to create the total effect, and each plays a role in the poem's essential meaning.

Awareness of the care and attention that poets give to composition helps guide your reading and adds an extra dimension to your understanding.

CHAPTER SEVEN

Hearing the Voices in the Poem

ho are you? That question has a number of answers. You can say that you're a person, a high school student, a son or a daughter, a sports enthusiast, a friend, a member of the photo club or debate team, and much more. Add to that what you'd like to become and what you can be in your imagination—and the possibilities are endless.

A poet is many people, too. And the voice of a poet may differ greatly from poem to poem. It may differ in tone (serious or light), in subject (wildflowers or war), and in attitude (mocking or mournful).

The voice you hear in a poem isn't the same as the voice a poet uses in everyday life—in asking directions, ordering a meal, expressing surprise, making an apology. In fact, conveying tone is difficult in poetry. When you speak, on the other hand, tone is difficult to conceal.

Like a musical instrument, the human voice can vary its tone to be full or reedy, booming or shrill, soft or harsh. And different tones of voice express a person's attitude—angry or awestruck, cheerful or melancholy.

A poet must find ways to express tone without the sound of a human voice and, through tone, make you aware of the attitude being expressed.

A Feeling of Aliveness

Read the following poem to discover how William Wordsworth achieves the tone that fits his advice about learning from nature. In making his point, Wordsworth uses the technique of *personification,* giving human qualities and characteristics to nonhuman things, like the sun and nature. For example, he writes

> Let Nature be your teacher
> She has a world of ready wealth.

Who's *she?* Trace back and you'll see that *she* is nature, whom Wordsworth personifies as a teacher. Wordsworth does this in three ways: by capitalizing Nature like a person's name, by using the pronoun *she,* and by calling Nature a teacher. Of course, you can't accept Nature as literally a woman and a teacher. But personification conveys a sense of how things seem. Often, a machine—a car, for example—will seem to have a personality. Everyone knows this isn't really possible, but it still seems to be so. And it is this feeling of aliveness that a poet hopes to convey through personification.

As you read, watch for other examples of personification and decide what their use contributes to the poem's meaning.

The Tables Turned

Up! Up! my friend, and quit your books;
Or surely you'll grow double:
Up! Up! my friend, and clear your looks;
Why all this toil and trouble?

The sun, above the mountain's head,   5
A freshening lustre mellow
Through all the long, green fields has spread,
His first sweet evening yellow.

Books! 'tis a dull and endless strife:*
Come, hear the woodland linnet,*   10
How sweet his music! on my life,
There's more of wisdom in it.

And hark! how blithe* the throstle* sings!
He, too, is no mean* preacher:
Come forth into the light of things,   15
Let Nature be your teacher.

She has a world of ready wealth,
Our minds and hearts to bless,—
Spontaneous* wisdom breathed by health,
Truth breathed by cheerfulness.   20

One impulse from a vernal* wood
May teach you more of man,
Of moral evil and of good,
Than all the sages* can.

Sweet is the lore* which Nature brings;   25
Our meddling intellect
Misshapes the beauteous forms of things,—
We murder to dissect.

Enough of Science and of Art;
Close up those barren* leaves;   30
Come forth, and bring with you a heart
That watches and receives.

——William Wordsworth

9. strife: struggle. **10. linnet:** a songbird. **13. blithe:** cheerful. **throstle:** a literary word for the song thrush. **14. mean:** poor, ineffective. **19. spontaneous:** coming effortlessly. **21. vernal:** springtime. **24. sages:** wise men. **25. lore:** lesson; learning. **30. barren:** unprofitable, lacking results.

FOCUSING IN

Write your answers on a separate piece of paper.

1. The speaker's tone is
   a. serious and commanding
   b. cheerful and lively
   c. thoughtful and melancholy
   d. unsure and uneasy.

2. The question in line 4 clarifies that "clear your looks" must mean
   a. wipe off that smile
   b. wash your face
   c. stop staring at me
   d. brighten up.

3. The *you* in this poem is most clearly the speaker's
   a. double self
   b. teacher
   c. friend
   d. son.

4. The time of day in the poem is
   a. sunrise
   b. high noon
   c. midafternoon
   d. early evening.

5. To bring nature to life, in stanza 2 the poet personifies the
   a. sun
   b. mountain
   c. fields
   d. evening.

6. In line 12 the speaker means there's more wisdom in
   a. a bird's song than in books
   b. music than in conflict
   c. coming than in going
   d. studying than in being bored doing nothing.

7. In addition to calling Nature a teacher, what other example of personification is used in stanza 4?

8. From stanza 5 list two kinds of "ready wealth" gained from being outdoors.

9. Line 28, "We murder to dissect," means
   a. people enjoy destroying and polluting nature
   b. people are killed for the savage fun of causing pain
   c. things get torn apart in the name of study or research
   d. choosing books over nature is like suicide.

10. "Barren leaves" must be the leaves of
    a. the table
    b. grass
    c. trees
    d. books.

Drawing Conclusions

A good part of reading involves making connections and seeing relationships that aren't spelled out. It's a mark of the poet's art to show, not tell—to let you draw the conclusions.

In the following examples, explain the character trait demonstrated by the behavior described.

1. A woman sees a little boy alone and crying in a shopping mall, takes him to the manager's office, and waits till his mother comes.

2. A girl receives a penalty for her behavior in class but doesn't try to excuse it by blaming others, too.

3. The winner of an essay contest credits his father with providing helpful suggestions for revision.

4. Someone scrawls a nasty comment and defaces a candidate's photo on a poster for the student senate election.

5. A girl decides not to pick the season's first rose because it looks so pretty on the bush.

Compare your conclusions with those of others in your class. Although details may differ, you'll probably agree on the basics.

Creating Actions

Choose five of the character traits listed below (or make up your own) and write a sentence or paragraph that illustrates those traits.

EXAMPLE:
Traits: stingy and dishonest
Sentence: While the others went ahead, Jeff scooped up the tips they had left and put them in his pocket.

1. trustworthy and reliable
2. thoughtless and inconsiderate
3. generous and unselfish
4. deceitful and sneaky
5. cowardly and disloyal
6. proud and truthful
7. kind and forgiving
8. courageous and steadfast
9. greedy and uncaring
10. thoughtful and sensitive

How Much Do Actions Show?

To *forbear* means "to hold back from doing something or to show restraint." In the following poem, "Forbearance," Ralph Waldo Emerson asks a series of questions, each containing an example that illustrates the trait of holding back.

In your first reading, try to determine the tone of the speaker and his relationship to someone called *thou*. Does the tone seem critical? Snoopy? Hopeful? Bitter? What in the poem leads to your conclusion?

Spot the instances of restraint that the speaker wonders about, and decide what character trait each illustrates.

Forbearance

Hast thou named all the birds without a gun?
Loved the wood-rose, and left it on its stalk?
At rich men's tables eaten bread and pulse?*
And loved so well a high behavior,
In man or maid, that thou from speech refrained,*   5
Nobility more nobly to repay?
O, be my friend, and teach me to be thine!

———Ralph Waldo Emerson

3. pulse: a thick soup or pottage made from peas, beans, lentils, etc. **5. refrained:** held back.

THINKING IT THROUGH

1. Who is the *thou* in this poem—an acquaintance of the speaker or anyone who can honestly answer ''yes'' to the speaker's questions?

2. What four specific actions does the speaker mention?

3. What character traits are illustrated by the examples in lines 1 and 2?

4. What desirable quality is at the heart of the behavior described in line 3?

5. What character trait is introduced in line 4? Why is it more appropriate here than earlier in the poem?

6. ''Loved...high behavior'' is an echo of ''loved the wood-rose.'' In what way is refraining from speech like leaving the wood-rose on its stalk?

7. Note that the poem has only two adjectives. How does this help illustrate the poet's purpose?

8. Emerson states that not praising high behavior is the more noble way to repay nobility. Explain his meaning, including the assumed purpose of a noble act.

9. Note that the words ''hast thou'' are not repeated, although they serve as understood words in other lines. Explain how this contributes to the poem's meaning and effect.

10. How does the last line differ from the preceding lines? Why is an exclamation point preferable to a period at the end? Discuss the difference made if the poem ended ''and gladly I'll be thine!''

A Sudden Insight

At what age do you classify a person as really old? What physical characteristics fit your image of old age? Can you list five? Ten? More?

Write as many as you can, and then compare your list with those of your classmates. After creating a master list, see whether your traits are included in the following poem. Like many poems, this one depends on your sharing a common body of knowledge and knowing the physical traits associated with old age.

Does a child's view of age differ from an adult's? With the words "I used to think...," poet Frances Cornford invites you to step back into childhood and share the insight the speaker gained.

Childhood

I used to think that grown-up people chose
To have stiff backs and wrinkles round their nose,
And veins like small fat snakes on either hand,
On purpose to be grand.
Till through the banisters* I watched one day   5
My great-aunt Etty's friend who was going away,
And how her onyx* beads had come unstrung.
I saw her grope to find them as they rolled;
And then I knew that she was helplessly old,
As I was helplessly young.   10

——Frances Cornford

5. **banisters:** the posts supporting the handrail of a staircase. 7. **onyx:** a type of quartz, often used in jewelry.

THINKING IT THROUGH

1. The phrase "I used to think" refers to the speaker's attitude at an earlier age. What are the only words that describe the speaker as a child?

2. By stating "I used to think," what does the speaker reveal about her attitude toward this incident and its importance to her?

3. What are three details the speaker once thought were physical characteristics of "grown-up" people? What might have led her to this conclusion?

4. What did the speaker once believe was the reason "grown-up people" looked old and wrinkled?

5. What in lines 1–4 explains why the child felt this way? How must the grown-ups have acted toward her?

6. Where was the child, while watching great-aunt Etty's friend pick up the beads? Why is this important to the poem?

7. *Grope* means "to feel about with the hands, to search blindly or uncertainly." How does Cornford's choice of this word describe more than one characteristic of old age?

8. Compare lines 1 and 9. What mistaken conclusion had the speaker reached about "grown-up people"? What is the difference between being grown-up and old?

9. Repeating the word *helplessly* shows the realization that both childhood and old age are alike in at least one respect. How are both helpless?

10. What conclusions about the comparison of different ages can you draw from the poem?

Getting in the Game

There are skills and strategies in baseball that a casual spectator never suspects. That's true of Robert Francis's poem "The Base Stealer," too. In both baseball and poetry, the more you know, the more you see. That goes double here. But you needn't be a baseball fan, just a keen observer, to participate in this poem.

After using the subject as the title, the poet never names the base stealer again. And note how long the poet waits to call the subject *he*. Waiting for the right moment is the key to stealing bases, and it's important to this poem as well.

Try to catch where and how the poet switches off from the usual use of punctuation. See if you can figure out why.

At first glance, some might say this poem's form has the squared-off shape of the base where the runner is safe. But there's much more to "The Base Stealer" than that. It's a poem that needs to be read aloud. When you do, you'll find yourself taking part in the action. Look closely at—or better still, listen to—how Robert Francis uses the sounds of words to show how it feels to be on base, steeling yourself to beat the throw.

The Base Stealer

Poised between going on and back,pulled
Both ways taut* like a tightrope-walker,
Fingertips pointing the opposites,
Now bouncing tiptoe like a dropped ball
Or a kid skipping rope, come on, come on,   5
Running a scattering of steps sidewise,
How he teeters, skitters, tingles, teases,
Taunts them, hovers like an ecstatic bird,
He's only flirting, crowd him, crowd him,
Delicate, delicate, delicate, delicate—now!   10

——Robert Francis

2. **taut:** strained, tense.

THINKING IT THROUGH

1. The subject of this poem is named in the title and not named again, or even called *he* until line 7. How does this delay affect the reading of the poem?

2. What effect is created by running the entire poem together in one sentence? How does this fit the poet's purpose?

3. Besides *skitters,* what other light, skittering kinds of words describe the player's motion? In lines 6–8, how does Francis use the sounds of words to create changes of pace?

4. Compare the following with the poem's first two lines. Explain why Francis's version is better. Consider sound and word placement.

   Poised between going on and back,
   Pulled both ways taut like a tightrope-walker.

5. In keeping with the words *pulled* and *taut,* how does the choice of words in line 3 add to the effect?

6. How does "dropped ball" illustrate a bounce? What is the difference in the way you say these two words together, compared to "drop the ball"? Which phrase is easier to say? Why?

7. Who is saying, "come on, come on," and "crowd him, crowd him"? Is it the narrator, the base stealer, or voices in the crowd? How do these comments add to the poem's effect?

8. How does the sound of the repeated word *delicate* in line 10 help the reader picture the base stealer at this moment?

9. What happens at the same time as the last word *now?*

10. The poem does not reveal whether the player was tagged out or was safe, so the poet must not think it important. What, then, did the poet want the reader to feel?

Taking Another Look

Here is a poet you've already met, adopting a different form and tone. In spite of the differences, you should be able to discern an attitude toward life and nature that's similar in both poems.

An important factor in determining tone is identifying the speaker's intended audience. Is it the reader? A friend or loved one? The speaker might be addressing an inanimate object, like a rose or a wave. Or the speaker could be talking to himself or herself.

In Wordsworth's poem "The Tables Turned," the speaker is clearly directing someone to "quit your books...and clear your looks." And although you, too, may take the advice to heart, it's addressed to someone the speaker calls "my friend."

Wordsworth begins the following poem, "The world is too much with us." Whom does he mean by "us?" What are the speaker's tone and attitude? To clarify your answers, be sure to check the setting and the person the speaker is addressing. Identifying one or two elements of a poem can lead to understanding others.

The World Is Too Much with Us

The world is too much with us; late and soon,
Getting and spending, we lay waste our powers;
Little we see in Nature that is ours;
We have given our hearts away, a sordid boon!*
This sea that bares her bosom to the moon;   5
The winds that will be howling at all hours,
And are upgathered now like sleeping flowers,
For this, for everything, we are out of tune;
It moves us not.—Great God! I'd rather be
A Pagan* suckled in a creed* outworn;   10
So might I, standing on this pleasant lea,*
Have glimpses that would make me less forlorn;
Have sight of Proteus rising from the sea;
Or hear old Triton blow his wreath'd horn.

—William Wordsworth

4. sordid boon: worthless token. **10. Pagan:** a member of a religion worshiping many gods. **creed:** set of beliefs. **11. lea:** pasture.

FOCUSING IN

Answer the following questions on a separate sheet of paper.

1. The word *world* is used as the opposite of
   a. society
   b. the universe
   c. heaven
   d. nature.

2. *We* should be taken to include the speaker and
   a. a friend nearby
   b. everyone, past and present
   c. the educated elite
   d. others like himself.

3. The setting invites you to picture the speaker
   a. sitting in his study
   b. looking out his office window
   c. giving a sermon in church
   d. standing, looking at the sea.

4. Write the exact words that serve as clues to your answer for question 3.

5. The speaker's words are directed to
   a. a friend
   b. himself
   c. his congregation
   d. Proteus and Triton.

6. The tone of "The World Is Too Much with Us" is
   a. serious and commanding
   b. cheerful and lively
   c. thoughtful and melancholy
   d. unsure and uneasy.

7. In the context of the poem, the powers laid waste are those of
   a. making money
   b. health and youth
   c. enjoying poetry, art, and culture
   d. appreciating nature.

8. "Late and soon" contains the idea of something
   a. that should happen shortly
   b. long continuing
   c. that should stop
   d. tardy and early.

9. The phrase "sordid boon" refers to
   a. bosom
   b. world
   c. hearts
   d. Pagan.

10. *Sordid* means "vile, filthy, mercenary—motivated solely by desire for material gain." What phrase in the poem supports this interpretation?

11. Copy two examples of personification.

12. The word that does not fit with a list of "everything" with which "we are out of tune" is
    a. the world
    b. the moon
    c. this sea
    d. the winds.

13. In the phrase "It moves us not," *moves* means
    a. teaches a moral lesson
    b. causes an emotional response
    c. answers questions
    d. makes to go away.

14. "Great God" serves all of the following purposes but one:
    a. an attention-getting device
    b. an introduction to a new line of thought
    c. an emphasis of the contrast between two creeds
    d. proof that the poet did become a pagan.

15. The word *Pagan* is a clue that Proteus and Triton must be
    a. islands
    b. gods
    c. sea monsters
    d. seashells.

16. The speaker states "I'd rather be/ A Pagan suckled in a creed outworn." The allusions to Proteus and Triton show he is referring to a belief such as
    a. the teachings of Buddhism
    b. an acknowledgment of atheism
    c. one held in ancient Greece
    d. the truth of astrological forecasts.

17. To the speaker, being a pagan seems better than
    a. serving a bad king
    b. being a poor person with rich friends
    c. seeing nothing valuable in nature
    d. suffering from a broken heart.

18. The phrases "have glimpses" and "have sight of" tie directly to what phrase earlier in the poem?

19. The glimpses of Proteus and Triton are symbolic of the speaker's desire to
    a. escape the fact of his failure
    b. regain a feeling of mystery and wonder in nature
    c. relive his past
    d. rid himself of guilt.

The Apostrophe

"Go, lovely Rose…"

From this line alone, it's impossible to be sure whether the speaker is telling a woman named Rose to go away or talking to a flower! Or both?

Edmund Waller's poem "Song" is an example of an apostrophe. In this sense, the word doesn't mean a mark of punctuation. Here apostrophe has an entirely different meaning. It is a poem in which *you* is a personified object or idea, addressed as a human being.

Flowers often carry messages. As you read the following poem, think of the reasons that the speaker asks a rose to deliver this one.

Song

Go, lovely Rose,
Tell her that wastes her time and me,
   That now she knows,
When I resemble* her to thee,
How sweet and fair she seems to be.   5

Tell her that's young,
And shuns to have her graces spied,
   That hadst thou sprung
In deserts, where no men abide,*
Thou must have uncommended* died.   10

Small is the worth
Of beauty from the light retired;*
   Bid her come forth,
Suffer* herself to be desired,
And not blush so to be admired.   15

Then die! that she
The common fate of all things rare
   May read in thee;
How small a part of time they share
That are so wondrous sweet and fair!   20

——Edmund Waller

---

4. resemble: compare. **9. abide:** make their homes. **10. uncommended:** without praise or notice. **12. retired:** withdrawn, removed. **14. suffer:** allow, permit.

THINKING IT THROUGH

1. If *you* is a personified rose, who is *her?* How does the first line express her behavior and attitude toward the speaker?

2. How does saying she "wastes" him, not his time, contrast his state of mind with hers? How does stanza 1 specifically compare her to the rose?

3. Does stanza 2 make her seem basically conceited, shy, or flirtatious? What leads to this conclusion? What would happen to a rose abloom in the desert?

4. How do the first two lines of stanza 3 reinforce the idea expressed in the previous stanza?

5. What three things should the rose "bid her" to do?

6. What does line 14 suggest is the purpose of such beauty as she and the rose possess?

7. How do lines 17 and 18 prove that the phrase "Then die" isn't meant to wish evil to her? What does the speaker want her to read into the fate of the rose?

8. In line 19 who are "they"? How are both alike?

9. How does line 20 echo the last line of stanza 1? The poet now feels free to add the word *wondrous*. What proves they deserve to be considered wonderful?

10. What idea about beauty does the poem illustrate through the symbol of the rose?

EXPERIMENTING WITH WORDS AND IDEAS

Making the right connections—and knowing when there isn't a reasonable one—is a requirement for logical thinking and clear-headed reading.

Four of the five items in each of the following lists share a common quality. Read each list carefully and decide which one doesn't fit. After you have noted the connection that links each set, see if you can think of more examples to add to each list.

EXAMPLE:
inky finger, badge, stuffed bear, revolver, desk.
Conclusion: The stuffed bear does not logically fit with the others, which might be items found in a police station. Other connected words are *traffic tickets, mug shots, handcuffs*.

1. steam, gas, steel, horse, water

2. shell, trap, fang, odor, spots

3. air, daisy, eggs, start, clock

4. sand, stars, cards, palm, tea leaves

5. onion, apple, happiness, pain, news

A Difference of Dirges

Each of the next two poems calls itself a dirge, but they could hardly be more different.

A dirge is a formal song of mourning and grief, and poets sometimes use the term to introduce expressions of sorrow and sadness...although not necessarily, as you'll see.

"Dirge" by Percy Bysshe Shelley apostrophizes six natural elements before the speaker bids them join in expressing grief. As you read, identify the six and determine their common factor.

Dirge

Rough wind, that moanest loud
  Grief too sad for song;
Wild wind, when sullen cloud
  Knells* all the night long;
Sad storm, whose tears are vain,   5
Bare woods, whose branches strain,
Deep caves and dreary main,*—
  Wail, for the world's wrong!

————Percy Bysshe Shelley

4. **knells:** gives forth a mourning, ominous sound. 7. **main:** open ocean, high sea.

FOCUSING IN

1. The elements are addressed six times in this apostrophe. List these elements, and explain what they have in common.

2. How do the adjectives describing these elements fit with the definition of a dirge?

3. After the first four elements, the poem states what each is doing. Briefly describe how the poet personifies each.

4. The final line could be paraphrased in two ways:

> Cry your grief loudly, because the world is wrong!
>
> *or*
>
> Cry your grief loudly, because of the wrong and injustice in the world.

How do the two versions differ in intent? Which seems to fit more logically with the rest of the poem? In what sense do both apply?

5. What is Shelley's purpose in apostrophizing six elements instead of choosing one or two?

Look at the hated things listed in the first stanza of the following poem. They should give you an idea of what's coming. What do they have in common, except being uncommon choices for pet hates? Get into the rhythm! Catch the tone of the speaker's voice! Do you really expect this to be a genuine dirge?

A Sea Dirge

There are certain things—as, a spider, a ghost,
　The income tax, gout,* an umbrella for three—
That I hate, but the thing that I hate the most
　Is a thing they call the Sea.

Pour some salt water over the floor—　　　　　　5
　Ugly I'm sure you'll allow it to be;
Suppose it extended a mile or more,
　That's very like the Sea.

Beat a dog till he howls outright—
　Cruel, but all very well for a spree;*　　　　　10
Suppose that he did so day and night,
　That would be like the Sea.

I had a vision of nurserymaids;
　Tens of thousands passed by me—
All leading children with wooden spades,　　　　15
　And this was by the Sea.

---

2. gout: disease causing painful swelling, especially of the big toe. **10. spree:** a free run of having fun.

(continued on next page)

Who invented those spades of wood?
  Who was it cut them out of the tree?
None, I think, but an idiot could—
  Or one that loved the Sea.   20

It is pleasant and dreamy, no doubt, to float
  With "thoughts as boundless, and souls as free";
But, suppose you are very unwell in the boat—
  How do you like the Sea?

There is an insect that people avoid   25
  (Whence is derived the verb "to flee").
Where have you been by it most annoyed?
  In lodgings by the Sea.

If you like your coffee with sands for dregs,
  A decided hint of salt in your tea,   30
And a fishy taste in the very eggs—
  By all means choose the Sea.

And if, with these dainties to drink and eat,
  You prefer not a vestige* of grass or tree,
And a chronic state of wet in your feet,   35
  Then—I recommend the Sea.

For *I* have friends who dwell by the coast—
  Pleasant friends they are to me!
It is when I am with them I wonder most
  That anyone likes the Sea.   40

They take me a walk; though tired and stiff
  To climb the heights I madly agree;
And after a tumble or so from the cliff,
  They kindly suggest the Sea.

I try the rock, and I think it cool   45
  That they laugh with such excess of glee,
As I heavily slip into every pool,
  That skirts the cold, cold sea.

                          ——Lewis Carroll

---

34. vestige: sign or trace.

THINKING IT THROUGH

Can you blame friends for laughing? Getting yourself laughed at isn't always easy, but this Lewis Carroll poem reads like a model for success.

Look for the humorous touches in each stanza and decide what makes them seem funny.

1. What items seem unexpected or out of place on a list of pet hates? Can you think of good reasons for hating the five things listed in lines 1 and 2? How does this stanza reveal the tone of the poem and the attitude you're expected to have toward the speaker's hatred of the sea?

2. What is wrong with the comparison the speaker uses in stanza 2? Why would the poet intentionally use a poor comparison?

3. How is the sea like a howling dog? How is it different? How do you know the poet can't be serious?

4. How much has the speaker exaggerated in stanza 4? Describe your version of the speaker's vision. How must the children with wooden spades feel about being part of this great horde?

5. Stanza 5 contains two questions that the speaker answered for himself. What answer would you have given? What makes the speaker's answer funny? Judging by line 19, what does the speaker consider "one that loved the Sea" to be?

6. How would you answer the question in stanza 6? How does that answer set up a contrast between it and the stanza's first two lines?

7. What kind of play on words is the basis for the humor in stanza 7? Is it true that the two "flees" are words related in their origin? Attack or defend the speaker's claim.

8. How do you know the speaker is simply pretending seriousness in stanza 8?

9. In stanza 9, what are "these dainties"? Why is the word *dainties* ironical? What other irony can you find in this stanza?

10. Why would the speaker "wonder most" about people liking the sea when he is with people he considers "pleasant friends"?

11. Why is "madly" an apt choice to describe the speaker's decision to "climb the heights"? How does it show the speaker making fun of himself? What word in line 44 shows irony? To what effect?

12. Who or what is the real target of the poem's humor? Why isn't the speaker's attitude reasonable? Even though the poem is making fun of the speaker's attitude, how is it similar to many people's feelings about something, if not the sea?

13. Can you think of any examples of "pet hates" that might be handled in a similar fashion? How are people's attitudes in such cases unreasonable?

On Your Own

Write your reactions to the songlike quality of the poem below. Whose voices do you hear?

Ballad of the Gypsy

I went to the Gypsy's.
Gypsy settin' all alone.
I said, Tell me, Gypsy,
When will my gal be home?

Gypsy said, Silver,   5
Put some silver in my hand
And I'll look into the future
And tell you all I can.

I crossed her palm with silver
Then she started in to lie.   10
She said, Now, listen, Mister,
She'll be here by and by.

    Aw, what a lie!

I been waitin' and a-waitin'
And she ain't come home yet.   15
Something musta happened
To make my gal forget.

Uh! I hates a lyin' Gypsy
Will take good money from you,
Tell you pretty stories   20
And take your money from you—

But if I was a Gypsy
I would take your money, too.

——Langston Hughes

Expressing Your Ideas

Choose a place that is special to you: at home, at school, where you go for vacation, where you work, where you go to have fun—or where you go to be by yourself. Make connections between this place and you.

- List at least five things (concrete nouns) you associate with this place.

- List at least five actions (verbs) that you do or that are done there.

- List at least five descriptive words (adjectives) that will fit this place precisely.

Use your list of associations as the basis for a descriptive paragraph or poem that helps your reader understand and share your feelings for this special place. You may use any or all of the words from your list in your finished writing.

Summing Up

When you read poetry, it's important to approach each poem with a fresh attitude and be ready for a fresh start.

Just because one poet uses the moon as a symbol of love doesn't mean the next one will. This time it may stand for loneliness...or something else. The same poet may express a lighthearted attitude in one poem...and deep gloom in the next.

When beginning each poem, familiarize yourself with the territory and look for important landmarks. Be sure to identify the speaker and find clues to attitude and tone. Being in tune with the poet's voice makes understanding easier.

Understanding the Story Behind the Story

oth *byte* and *astronaut* are terms dealing with modern technologies. They symbolize two extremes in the ways that words come into use.

> **byte:** a unit of information for processing in computers.
> **astronaut:** a person engaged in or trained for space flight.

Byte is a coined word, one made up to fill a special need. It was invented to name a new piece of computer technology carrying a unit of information. It's a word without a past, lacking related words and widely accepted connotations.

Astronaut is very different. It comes from two words reaching back to ancient Greece. *Astro* means "of the stars." *Naut* means "of or about sailors." So astronauts are really sailors to the stars, continuing a long line of fearless sailors who set out when the Mediterranean Sea was a mystery and the oceans of Earth were never before crossed.

Words, like trees, develop layers as they grow over time. Because words are the tools of their trade, poets respect these layers of meaning and use a word's nuances, shades, and variations of sense to color their poetry and give it richness and depth.

Knowing a word's origin often helps you see it in a clearer and more precise light.

Layers of Meaning

Advertisers tend to ignore word origins, preferring to exaggerate the size, value, quality, usefulness, and beauty of what they have for sale.

Here are seven adjectives, all descriptive of something huge or bigger than ordinary. They are commonly used in advertising, but their backgrounds show what different nuances they really possess.

a. **colossal:** from a word referring to a gigantic statue. The original Colossus was one of the seven wonders of the ancient world.

b. **tremendous:** contains the sense of being dreadful, causing to shake or quake. Related words are *tremble, tremor,* and *tremulous.*

c. **gargantuan:** Gargantua was a fictional giant and king. In spite of his huge size, he was a good-natured man who loved to eat and drink.

d. **monumental:** worth comparing to a monument, either because of size, historical importance, or both.

e. **enormous:** differing from the normal (*e-norm*); greatly exceeding or going beyond the normal size.

f. **immense:** (*im + mensus:* not + measure) This "big" word is so big that it can hardly be measured. It seems to have no boundaries.

g. **titanic:** According to myth, the Titans were beings of enormous size, strength, and power who populated Earth before the coming of human beings.

Match one of these adjectives to each of the following descriptions, choosing the one with a nuance that you feel fits best. There may be more than one suitable choice. Have a reason to back up your decision. Write your answers on a separate sheet of paper.

1. An 800-page novel with an entertaining, easy-to-read plot.

2. A planned undertaking to create international understanding and cooperation.

3. A new sports stadium with the country's largest seating capacity.

4. An earthquake that covers much territory and causes much damage.

5. Company profits far greater than expected.

6. A movie with a "cast of thousands" and a plot based on an epic tale.

7. A conflict requiring superhuman heroism and strength.

8. A research project of a size and scope never before attempted.

9. A huge beast that looks fiercer than it really is (use the noun form of adjective given).

10. An intercontinental ballistic missile named to indicate strength and power (noun).

Poetry as Experience

One sense of *terrible* is "causing great terror or fear." In this regard, Stephen Spender's poem sets out to be terrible. Spender, an English poet born in 1909, lived through two world wars. "A Man-Made World" recreates a wartime event and asks its reader to share the experience of taking shelter during an air raid.

A Man-Made World

What a wild room
We enter, when the gloom
Of windowless night
Shuts us from the light

In a black, malicious* box.   5
A freezing key locks
Us into utter dark
Where the nerves hark*

For the man-made toys
To begin their noise.   10
The siren wails. After,
Broomsticks climb through air,

Then clocks burst through their springs,
Then the fire-bell rings.
Above and below comes   15
The anger of the drums.

Oh, what white rays gleaming
Against the sky's crouched* ceiling!
What sudden flashes show
A woman who cries Oh!   20

5. malicious: filled with a desire to cause injury or suffering, especially when based on deep-rooted meanness. **8. hark:** listen, wait to hear. **18. crouched:** bent or stooped low, especially from fear or as a sign of submission.

(continued on next page)

In darkness where we are
With no saving star,
We hear the world we made
Pay back what we paid:

Money, steel, fire, stones,   25
Stripping flesh from bones,
With a wagging tongue of fear
Tormenting the ear,

Knocking at the outer skin,
To ask if any soul is in,   30
While the gloom descends
On our means* become our ends.

—Stephen Spender

32. means: method, instrument, that by which something is done or obtained.

THINKING IT THROUGH

Anyone who has not survived an air raid or lived in a war-torn country may be unable to experience fully the feelings Spender describes. Yet part of the reason for reading poetry is to expand one's emotional horizons, to stretch and grow in feeling by entering into another's consciousness.

As you discuss questions about "A Man-Made World," remember the poem concerns an intense experience that in some cases allows a variety of interpretations.

1. "Wild room . . . windowless night . . . black box . . . utter dark." During air raids and blackouts, street lights were extinguished. Civilians hid in shelters or draped their windows tightly shut so no trace of light escaped to guide enemy bombers. After a series of raids, why might one call the room "wild" and compare it to a "malicious" box?

2. What is unusual about Spender's division of this poem into stanzas? What effect is achieved by this?

3. What "man-made toys" must the listeners be waiting to hear?

4. In lines 12–16 Spender uses ordinary objects as symbols instead of listing weapons, bombs, and other implements of war. List the four common objects named and the things connected with war they could represent.

5. Stanzas 3 and 4 are examples of ironic understatement, purposely presented less strongly than the facts seem to allow. What must be Spender's purpose for not calling a bomb a bomb?

6. In line 20 the sudden flashes could show a woman "who screams No-o-o!" instead of one "who cries Oh!" How would the effect be different? Which is more effective and why?

7. Line 23 holds the third reference to a world made by man. Where are the other two? How does this contrast with the usual concept people have concerning how the world was made? What must be meant by "no saving star"?

8. The last two stanzas let loose terrors that settle the account and are the violent repayment that humanity has brought on itself. How is each of the four things in line 25 involved with war? What parts of the human body does Spender list in lines 26 to 29? What feelings and sensations does he associate with each?

9. After calling this a man-made world, why does the poem raise the question of a soul? In a poem about war, what must be "our means" and what must be "our ends"?

10. In line 32, "While the gloom descends" is an echo of stanza 1, "when the gloom . . . Shuts us from the light." How might gloom symbolize more than the dark during an air raid? Do you consider Spender's attitude too strong, or do you think it's a valid warning against war and its threat to humanity?

Giving Words Their Due

Read the definitions below, then the poem that follows, and discover how the poet plays upon the meanings of the two words.

> *idyll:* a short poem describing country life and suggesting a mood of peace and contentment
> *idle:* inactive, passing the time doing nothing

An Idle Idyll by a very Humble Member
of the Great and Noble London Mob

This is the Heath of Hampstead,*
There is the dome of Saint Paul's;
Beneath, on the serried* house-tops
A chequered* lustre* falls:

And the mighty city of London,   5
Under the clouds and the light,
Seems a low wet beach, half shingle*
With a few sharp rocks upright.

Here will we sit, my darling,
And dream an hour away: 10
The donkeys are hurried and worried,
But we are not donkeys today:

Through all the weary week, dear,
We toil in the murk* down there,
Tied to a desk and a counter,   15
A patient stupid pair!

But on Sunday we slip our tether,*
And away from the smoke and the smirch;*
Too grateful to God for his Sabbath
To shut its hours in a church.   20

Away to the green, green country,
Under the open sky;
Where the earth's sweet breath is incense
And the lark sings psalms on high.

On Sunday we're Lord and Lady,   25
With ten times the love and glee
Of those pale and languid rich ones
Who are always and never free.

They drawl and stare and simper,*
So fine and cold and staid,*   30
Like exquisite waxwork figures
That must be kept in the shade:

We can laugh out loud when merry,
We can romp at kiss-in-the-ring,
We can take our beer at a public,*   35
We can loll on the grass and sing. . . .

Would you grieve very much, my darling,
If all yon* low wet shore
Were drowned by a mighty flood-tide,
And we never toiled there more?   40

Wicked?—There is no sin, dear,
In an idle dreamer's head;
He turns the world topsy-turvy
To prove that his soul's not dead.

I am sinking, sinking, sinking;   45
It is hard to sit upright!
Your lap is the softest pillow!
Good night, my love, good night!

——James Thomson (from *Sunday at Hampstead*)

1. Hampstead Heath: a spot on the outskirts of London where working people liked to spend their days off. **3. serried:** placed closely together; marked by ridges, serrated. **4. chequered:** alternately light and shadow. **lustre:** radiance, shine. **7. shingle:** coarse gravel. **14. murk:** darkness and gloom. **17. tether:** a leash which limits the range of movement. **18. smirch:** soot, dust, dirt. **29. simper:** smile in a silly, self-conscious way. **30. staid:** proper, seriously well-mannered. **35. public:** public house, a British tavern. **38. yon:** yonder, over there.

FOCUSING IN

Write your answers on a separate sheet of paper.

1. The "we" in the poem refers to
   a. the speaker and reader
   b. all working people of London
   c. a workingman and his love
   d. the speaker and an impersonal *you.*

2. The occasion is
   a. the speaker's Sunday off
   b. lunch hour on a workday
   c. a reception for a Lord and Lady
   d. a flood of memories being recalled by an old man.

3. From the Heath of Hampstead, the city of London looks like
   a. a cloud of smirch and smog
   b. a mighty fortress
   c. a shining halo of light
   d. a low, wet, rocky beach

4. According to the speaker, most of their week is spent
   a. hurrying and worrying
   b. dreaming of becoming rich
   c. toiling patiently and wearily
   d. being grateful for having jobs.

5. Stanzas 5 and 6 show that the speaker believes that
   a. God and religion are of no importance
   b. it was sinful to slip away on Sunday
   c. enjoying nature is the best way to serve God
   d. they are too poor to dress properly for church.

6. Stanza 8 provides the proof of why the speaker feels people such as he
   a. deserve to be called dreamers and idlers
   b. have ten times the love and glee of the rich
   c. behave sinfully when they should be in church
   d. are always and never happy and free.

7. Among the things that the speaker dreams about is
   a. London's being drowned by a flood
   b. having fine and exquisite manners
   c. becoming the manager of his office
   d. getting a chance to rest in the shade, out of the seaside sun.

8. The poem draws a contrast between the speaker's considering himself to be patient, stupid, and donkey-like, yet
   a. able to grieve very much
   b. with a soul far from dead
   c. wicked and sinful
   d. idle unless forced to labor on weekdays.

9. In relation to stanzas 10 and 11, "I am sinking, sinking, sinking" seems to mean the speaker is
   a. drowning under the weight of his hard life
   b. overwhelmed by wickedness and sin
   c. going completely out of his mind
   d. hoping that his dreams have come true.

10. The last three lines show that the speaker
    a. is overwhelmed by illness
    b. makes a punning excuse to lay his head in his loved one's lap
    c. is daydreaming at his desk, instead of working
    d. intends to flee from London and live in the country.

Worlds in Words

Test your sensitivity to words by answering the following questions:

1. Which seems more common?

> Sandalwood or firewood
> Peacocks or railroad tracks
> Pig-lead or emeralds

2. Which seems more graceful?

> A sailing ship or a coal carrier
> A ship butting its way along or one rowing home to haven

3. Which seem more full of romance and the unknown?

> Palm-tree shores or the coast of England
> Ancient times or modern days
> Mad March weather or the climate of the Tropics

John Masefield uses comparisons like these as a basis for the following poem. Though some words may be foreign to your vocabulary, the choices you made in this exercise should lead you to see how he feels about the "Cargoes." People have long felt that the call of the sea was the call of adventure. Is this still so today?

Cargoes

Quinquireme* of Nineveh* from distant Ophir,*
Rowing home to haven in sunny Palestine,
With a cargo of ivory,
And apes and peacocks,
Sandalwood, cedarwood, and sweet white wine.   5

Stately Spanish galleon* coming from the isthmus,*
Dipping through the Tropics by the palm-tree shores,
With a cargo of diamonds,
Emeralds, amethysts,
Topazes, and cinnamon, and gold moidores.*   10

Dirty British coaster* with salt-caked smokestack,
Butting through the Channel* in the mad March days,
With a cargo of Tyne* coal,
Road-rails,* pig-lead,*
Firewood, ironware, and cheap tin trays.   15

——John Masefield

1. Quinquireme: a galley (rowed ship) with five separate sets of oarsmen.
Nineveh: ancient capital of Assyria on the Tigris River. **Ophir:** an ancient country,
probably located in Arabia. **6. galleon:** a large sailing ship, used principally by the
Spanish in the sixteenth and seventeenth centuries. **Isthmus:** a narrow strip of
land; Isthmus of Panama. **10. moidores:** gold coins of Portugal and Brazil.
11. coaster: a ship plying the coastal waters of a country. **12. Channel:** English
Channel between England and France. **13. Tyne:** river in northern England.
14. road-rails: sections of railroad tracks. **pig-lead:** oblong blocks of lead.

THINKING IT THROUGH

1. In what ways are all three stanzas alike?

2. "Cargoes" has no active verbs, although Masefield has the different craft "rowing," "dipping," and "butting." What effect does he create by using this form?

3. Masefield's use of unfamiliar vocabulary furthers the effect of the poem. Which stanza names the least-known places? Which lists the least-expected cargo?

4. Five of the six items carried by the Spanish galleon share a common quality. Which one doesn't fit? Why?

5. What negative words are used to describe the British coaster and its cargo?

6. Does distance in time and place make the first two ships seem more glamorous? Which really represents the better life: a ship rowed by oarsmen or one with a smokestack? Railroad tracks or sandalwood? Which kind of ship would you prefer to sail on? Why?

7. Why has Masefield chosen to call this poem "Cargoes"? What is the main conclusion that he wants you to draw from the poem's examples?

Words, Words, and More Words

One of the easiest ways to increase your vocabulary is to let one word help define another. Just start from what you know.

If you've heard the expression "sly as a fox," you should be able to figure out why a fox is *sycophantic*. You know a canary can sing, but can a raven? Knowing the answer will help you discover why the raven proved to be *gullible* in the following poem entitled "The Sycophantic Fox and the Gullible Raven." Maybe you don't know what *Brie* is or *Roquefort*. But if you read the following poem closely, checking the unfamiliar words against those you know, you should arrive at a general understanding of most of the unfamiliar words.

The Sycophantic Fox and the Gullible Raven

A raven sat upon a tree,
   And not a word he spoke, for
His beak contained a piece of Brie,
   Or, maybe, it was Roquefort.
      We'll make it any kind you please—   5
      At all events it was a cheese.

Beneath the tree's umbrageous limb
   A hungry fox sat smiling;
He saw the raven watching him,
   And spoke in words beguiling: 10
      "J'admire," said he, "ton beau plumage,"
      (The which was simply persiflage.)

Two things there are, no doubt you know,
   To which a fox is used:
A rooster that is bound to crow,   15
   A crow that's bound to roost:
      And whichsoever he espies
      He tells the most unblushing lies.

"Sweet fowl," he said, "I understand
   You're more than merely natty,   20
I hear you sing to beat the band
   And Adelina Patti.
      Pray render with your liquid tongue
      A bit from *Götterdämmerung*."

This subtle speech was aimed to please   25
   The crow, and it succeeded;
He thought no bird in all the trees
   Could sing as well as he did.
      In flattery completely doused,
      He gave the "Jewel Song" from *Faust*.   30

But gravitation's law, of course,
   As Isaac Newton showed it,
Exerted on the cheese its force,
   And elsewhere soon bestowed it.
      In fact, there is no need to tell   35
      What happened when to earth it fell.

I blush to add that when the bird
   Took in the situation
He said one brief, emphatic word,
   Unfit for publication.   40
     The fox was greatly startled, but
     He only sighed and answered "Tut."

The Moral is: A fox is bound
   To be a shameless sinner.
And also: when the cheese comes round   45
   You know it's after dinner.
     But (what is only known to few)
     The fox is after dinner too.

—Guy Wetmore Carryl

FOCUSING IN

Choose the correct definitions for the following words. (The lines in which the words appear are given in parentheses.) Write your answers on a separate piece of paper.

1. *Brie* and *Roquefort* (3,4) are kinds of
   a. trees
   b. cheese
   c. birds
   d. wild animals.

2. *Umbrageous* (7) means
   a. shady
   b. uneven
   c. shapely
   d. unusual.

3. "J'admire...ton beau plumage" (11) means
   a. You must weigh a ton
   b. I'd like to buy a plum
   c. I admire your beautiful feathers
   d. I'm a mere boy, not your age.

4. *Persiflage* (12) means
   a. playful, teasing remarks
   b. untranslatable language
   c. pangs of hunger
   d. words of wisdom.

5. *Adelina Patti* (22) must be a
   a. type of cake
   b. musical instrument
   c. sweet fowl
   d. singer.

6. *Götterdämmerung* (24) and *Faust* (30) are examples of
   a. swear words
   b. operas
   c. beers
   d. weapons.

7. *Bestowed* (34) means
   a. presented as a gift
   b. made to disappear
   c. threw
   d. caused to drop.

8. *Sycophantic* (title) means
   a. speaking foreign languages
   b. being evil and cannibalistic
   c. flattering for self-seeking reasons
   d. without genuine need or justification.

9. *Gullible* means
   a. incapable of singing
   b. easily gulled or tricked
   c. tending to gulp food
   d. being of unstable mentality.

EXPERIMENTING WITH WORDS AND IDEAS

Be ready to discuss the techniques Carryl uses to create the humor of "The Sycophantic Fox and the Gullible Raven."

Working in groups, find examples of such techniques as irony, exaggeration, and plays on words. Is there something basically funny about using big words to describe small events? What parts of the poem would you call most humorous? What seems most subtle or difficult to catch?

Record your conclusions, and compare your findings with those of the rest of your class.

The Rightness of the Poet's Choices

A good writer has a purpose for choosing a vague, nicer-sounding term in place of a blunt, more direct one. In "A Narrow Fellow in the Grass," the poet never directly names the subject. Why not? The answer to that question will guide you to the reaction the poet wants you to have.

What is the connotation of *fellow* in such expressions as *fellowship, fellow Americans,* and *fellow creatures*? What is the relationship among *fellow members* of a group? Think of this sense of the word as you read the poem.

A narrow fellow in the grass

A narrow fellow in the grass
Occasionally rides;
You may have met him—did you not?
His notice sudden is.

The grass divides as with a comb,   5
A spotted shaft is seen;
And then it closes at your feet
And opens further on.

He likes a boggy acre,
A floor too cool for corn.   10
Yet when a boy, and barefoot,
I more than once, at morn,

Have passed, I thought, a whip lash
Unbraiding in the sun,—
When, stopping to secure it,   15
It wrinkled, and was gone.

Several of nature's people
I know, and they know me;
I feel for them a transport
Of cordiality;*   20

But never met this fellow
Attended* or alone,
Without a tighter breathing,
And Zero at the Bone.

——Emily Dickinson

19–20. **transport of cordiality:** strong feeling of sympathy and kindness.
22. **attended:** with someone else.

THINKING IT THROUGH

1. What effect does the poet try to create by using the term "narrow fellow" instead of being more direct? How do many people feel about the creature which is the poem's subject?

2. In line 3, the speaker asks, "You may have met him—did you not?" Is *you* most likely to be the reader or someone accompanying the speaker? Use stanzas 1 and 2 as proof, including the tense of the verbs and the word *occasionally.* How is personification used in stanza 1?

3. It is unlikely that both *you* and the speaker should have met the same snake. Why then does the poet use the words *fellow* and *he,* instead of the more accurate *fellows* and *them*? What attitude is the poet attempting to create?

4. In lines 7 and 8, what is "it" that opens and closes? What effect or picture does this create?

5. Line 11 begins with "Yet" although the poet used "But" in earlier versions. What difference do you see between the two choices?

6. The poem describes its subject as riding, unbraiding, and wrinkling. How does each verb fit a snake's movements?

7. In line 17 the poet speaks of "nature's people." How does this phrase accurately express the speaker's feelings? How does it relate to the word *fellow*?

8. The speaker says he feels a "transport of cordiality." How does this explain the way he'd like to feel toward the snake?

9. What clues prove he can't wholeheartedly feel this way?

10. Suppose the following had been the last stanza.

> But never met this fellow,
> Whatever mood I'm in,
> Without a shiver up my spine,
> And Goosebumps on my Skin.

Why is this version less effective than the one the poet actually wrote? What makes "Zero at the Bone" more forceful?

Fabulous Reality

Just like philosophers, poets take on life's big ideas—love and hate, pride and envy. But poets have their own way of dealing with these ideas. Instead of expounding on theories, they use specific, concrete language. And they often use stories to illustrate their thoughts.

Remember "The Sycophantic Fox and the Gullible Raven" on page 154? It's typical of how poets handle big ideas—in this case, flattery and vanity. That kind of poem is called a *fable.* At first glance, it seems to be a poem about animals. But really it isn't. Personification—giving human characteristics to animals and lifeless objects—is often a mark of fables. The talking fox and silly raven represent people, and this poem is actually about human nature—about self-serving, empty praise and foolish conceit.

Fables approach reality through the unreal. But their stories often carry ideas worthy of a philosopher. As you read the following poetic fables, you'll discover "Once upon a time" is not always so simple as it seems!

The Flower

Once in a golden hour
   I cast to earth a seed.
Up there came a flower,
   The people said, a weed.

To and fro they went   5
   Thro' my garden-bower,*
And muttering discontent
   Cursed me and my flower.

Then it grew so tall
   It wore a crown of light,   10
But thieves from o'er the wall
   Stole the seed by night.

Sowed it far and wide
   By every town and tower,
Till all the people cried   15
   "Splendid is the flower."

---

6. bower: a leafy shelter, covered by vines or boughs.

(continued on next page)

Read my little fable:
   He that runs may read.
Most can raise the flower now,
   For all have got the seed.   20

And some are pretty enough,
   And some are poor indeed,
And now again the people
   Call it but a weed.

——Alfred, Lord Tennyson

THINKING IT THROUGH

Each stanza is a step in the story and represents a different characteristic of human nature.

1. What words show that the speaker felt that planting the seed was worthwhile? What accounts for the people's reaction? How is this typical of many people who encounter something they have never seen and know nothing about?

2. How would you expand the description of the action and attitude in stanza 2? How does this fit people's behavior when they feel threatened? Why would they curse when anger seems unnecessary?

3. What led the thieves to steal the seed?

4. Give two factors that could cause the people to change their minds and decide the flower was "splendid." How is this typical of human nature?

5. Line 18 seems a puzzlement. In line 17 who is being asked to "read my little fable"? What percentage of readers can probably run? If "raise the flower" means understanding the meaning of the fable, what would be the "seed"? Based on lines 18 and 20, to whom does this apply?

6. In the final stanza, people don't base their reaction on whether the flowers are pretty or not. On what do they base it? Why do they again decide the flower is just a worthless weed? What further characteristic of human nature does this show?

7. What is the point of the following poetic fable, and what does it say about people and the way they determine the value of possessions?

Fable

In heaven
Some little blades of grass
Stood before God.
"What did you do?"
Then all save one of the little blades   5
Began eagerly to relate
The merits of their lives.
This one stayed a small way behind,
Ashamed.

Presently, God said,   10
"And what did *you* do?"
 The little blade answered, "O my Lord,
Memory is bitter to me,
For if I did good deeds
I know not of them."   15
Then God, in all his splendor,
Arose from his throne.
"O best little blade of grass!" he said.

——Stephen Crane

FOCUSING IN

Working in pairs, discuss the human characteristics brought out in Crane's "Fable." In what way do blades of grass serve as a good choice to represent people coming before the heavenly throne? Why were all but one so eager to relate their merits?

What character traits is Crane criticizing in stanza 1? How?

In stanza 2, why might the little blade's memories be bitter, even after doing good deeds? Considering God's reaction, why is it likely the good deeds are many? Why isn't it necessary to convince God of one's merits? Is "not knowing" of good deeds the same as not doing them? What positive character traits does this "best little blade of grass" have?

What do you like or dislike about this poem? What words or phrases do you think are particularly effective? What questions, if any, need more consideration and discussion?

On Your Own

This is one of the world's most famous poetic fables. How does its story relate to human nature as you know it? Write your reactions to "A Poison Tree" in your notebook.

A Poison Tree

I was angry with my friend:
I told my wrath,* my wrath did end.
I was angry with my foe:
I told it not, my wrath did grow.

And I water'd it in fears,   5
Night and morning with my tears;
And I sunn'd it with smiles,
And with soft deceitful wiles.

And it grew both day and night,
Till it bore an apple bright;   10
And my foe beheld it shine,
And he knew that it was mine,

And into my garden stole
When the night had veil'd the pole:*
In the morning glad I see   15
My foe outstretch'd beneath the tree.

——William Blake

2. **wrath:** desire for revenge, resulting from anger. **14. pole:** Polaris, the North Star, polestar.

Another Taste of Hate

Without a Cloak

Hate has a fashionable cut.
  It is the garment man agrees on,
Snug, colorful, the proper weight
  For comfort in any icy season.

And it is weatherproof, they say—   5
  Becoming, also, to the spirit.
I fetched Hate homeward yesterday,
  But there it hangs. I cannot wear it.

It is a dress that suits me ill,
  However much the mode* sustains me.   10
At once too ample and too small,
  It trips, bewilders, and confines me.

And in my blood do fevers flow,
  Corruptive, where the fabric presses,
Till I must pluck it off as though   15
  It were the burning shirt of Nessus.*

Proud walk the people folded warm
  In Hate. They need not pray for spring.
But threadbare do I face the storm
  Or hug my hearthstone, shivering.   20

——Phyllis McGinley

10. mode: manner or fashion. **16. Nessus:** a mythological creature who gave Hercules a poisoned shirt that caused horrible agony and that couldn't be removed. To escape it, Hercules killed himself.

THINKING IT THROUGH

Compare "Without a Cloak" and "A Poison Tree" to see how one poem reinforces the other.

1. What are the basic metaphors of each poem? What qualities characteristic of hate are brought out by each metaphor?

2. List words used by each poet to show the attractions that hate has for people.

3. How do the two speakers differ in their willingness to accept hate into their lives? To indicate this, how is the metaphor carried out in each poem?

4. McGinley writes that hate is corruptive or corrupts. What in Blake's poem supports this idea?

5. In stanza 5 of "Without a Cloak," why does the speaker feel poorly prepared for the storm? For what is this a metaphor?

6. How does Blake's poem echo the idea that people "cloaked in hate" are proud and warm?

7. How does McGinley also develop the metaphor of poison being part of hate?

8. What in Blake's poem supports the concept that the speaker is emotionally poisoned by hatred and his passion to destroy his foe?

9. Which of the two metaphors do you find more effective? Why?

10. Which of the two poems do you prefer? Which do you find easier to understand? Be prepared to share and explain your opinions.

Summing Up

Practice. Know the rules. Be willing to take risks. That's the way to become better at reading poetry as well as playing a sport.

How do you handle an unfamiliar word? Many times you'll find clues to meaning right in the poem. By gaining confidence in your ability to understand unfamiliar words through their uses, you'll increase your vocabulary, add to your enjoyment, and become a better reader.

Words have many different origins. And most have layer upon layer of meaning, so the more you know about a word the more you'll find it saying. That's why poetry and language never stop giving you room to grow.

CHAPTER NINE

From the Known to the Unknown

What would you say was the hardest thing in the world to invent?

Think of the early human beings who discovered amazing uses for two straight sticks. Someone rubbed them together and made fire. Someone else wound, looped, and twisted wool around them—and created knitting. And another person manipulated them with one hand to pick up food—and invented chopsticks.

What other uses for a pair of straight sticks can you think of?

Some civilizations—advanced in other ways—never discovered a practical use for the wheel. Do you realize how many other inventions depend on this one?

And one of the greatest inventions of all was the concept of zero. You can easily identify one object. And you can count any number of objects one by one. But how do you count something that isn't there? How do you imagine a number for a thing that doesn't exist? Think of the difficulty of dreaming up something that stands for the absence of quantity—and inventing zero!

These and countless other inventions are so taken for granted today that they're hardly credited as inventions. Yet they represent the important first steps, often the most difficult, that led to more complex ones.

Real thinking and inventiveness come not from memorizing and repeating what you're told but from seeing relationships, getting ideas, and imagining possibilities that go beyond what you learn from others.

That's the challenge of poetry. There's no formula for solving its problems. You must meet each poem on its own terms.

That's the irony in the beginner's cry, "I don't understand it!" No one can expect to understand a good poem in an instant. Reading poetry is always an act of discovery. You must learn how to let the poem itself answer your questions.

And if poetry never becomes effortless to read, that's because it always holds something new.

Paying Attention to Word Order

Chocolate was an irresistible temptation for her.
For her chocolate was an irresistible temptation.
An irresistible temptation for her was chocolate.

These sentences contain the same words. Do they express exactly the same idea? Word order has an important effect on the way you perceive ideas from sentences and paragraphs, lines and stanzas.

In sentences, first and last words claim the most attention. And in English, subjects with their descriptive words and phrases usually come first. That's the case with the sentence below:

The solution to the mystery was right before his eyes.

But what about this?

Right before his eyes was the solution to the mystery.

The subject hasn't changed, only its placement, which makes it trickier to find. Then what about this version?

Right before his eyes, so obvious that he wondered
how he ever could have missed seeing it earlier, was the
solution to the mystery.

In many cases, word order and sentence construction, not vocabulary and ideas, make a poem seem difficult.

No matter how long, involved, and complicated a sentence appears at first, look for a basic sentence pattern. Be on the alert for introductory words signaling that the true subject of the sentence is coming later.

Consider these examples:

It is not bragging about yourself that shows you deserve admiration.

Bragging about yourself doesn't show you deserve admiration.

And what about the following?

When there is not enough time for him to spend on any other project and he has a few minutes to wait before it's time to leave the house, Jason sometimes plays a few hands of solitaire.

Were you waiting for something to happen after getting the signal from "When"? At the root of this sentence is the simple statement:

Jason sometimes plays a few hands of solitaire.

The introductory words, all twenty-nine of them, are only used to answer the question, When does Jason play solitaire?

EXPERIMENTING WITH WORDS AND IDEAS

On a separate sheet of paper, rewrite the following sentences in standard word order, putting the subject with its descriptive words first. If a sentence starts with *it,* eliminate the *it* and start with a more specific subject. If a sentence is already in standard order, simply write *standard* after its number.

1. Right at the edge of the table was perched a very breakable and expensive dish.

2. There at the window a sudden glare of a flashlight shines to attract our attention.

3. Give me advice on books to read that have exciting plots and movies to see with more action than romance.

4. Pushing and shoving to get inside, ignoring shouts to wait, rushes the incoming crowd.

5. After a while you will make much sense of this, and at that time you should its purpose see.

6. It is not every day that you see such an amazing sight as a green elephant with orange stripes.

7. Chocolate or strawberry, which one to choose as my favorite flavor, I find hard to decide.

8. As red is green, so right this is and wrong are you.

Finding the Way

In the following poem, "Smooth Between Sea and Land," A. E. Housman uses unusual word order to create a poem that should make you think. Read it once, noticing its key words and getting a basic feeling for what the poem is about. Then do a closer reading and decide how you would rephrase some of the trickier lines in standard word order.

If you have difficulty understanding some of the ideas, find the basic sentence pattern and work from what you know. For example, you could restate the first two lines as follows: The yellow sand is laid smooth between sea and land.

Smooth Between Sea and Land

Smooth between sea and land
Is laid the yellow sand
And here through summer days
The seed of Adam plays.

Here the child comes to found*   5
His unremaining mound,
And the grown lad to score*
Two names upon the shore.

Here, on the level sand,
Between the sea and land,   10
What shall I build or write
Against the fall of night?

Tell me of runes to grave*
That hold the bursting wave,
Or bastions* to design   15
For longer date than mine.

Shall it be Troy or Rome
I fence against the foam,
Or my own name to stay
When I depart for aye?*   20

Nothing: too near at hand,
Planing* the figured sand,
Effacing* clean and fast
Cities not built to last
And charms devised in vain,   25
Pours the confounding* main.*

——A. E. Housman

---

5. found: make, establish. **7. score:** mark with lines. **13. runes to grave:** magic signs to mark or engrave on the sand. **15. bastions:** strongholds. **20. for aye:** forever. **22. planing:** smoothing. **23. effacing:** wiping away. **26. confounding:** bringing to ruin or nothingness. **main:** the sea or ocean.

FOCUSING IN

Write your answers on a separate sheet of paper.

1. The first two lines focus your attention on the
   a. great expanse of the sea
   b. stretch of the horizon
   c. area of sandy shore
   d. vastness of earth's reaches.

2. "Seed of Adam" in line 4 refers to
   a. grains of sand being as old as Eden
   b. all children as descendants of Adam and Eve
   c. the evolution of creatures from the sea
   d. the contrast between the beach and the Garden of Eden.

3. In line 6 "His unremaining mound" is most likely
   a. a sand castle the waves will erase
   b. the grave of a drowned child
   c. the abandoned home of Adam and Eve
   d. an anthill the child destroys.

4. Lines 7 and 8 refer to
   a. the silliness of romantic lads
   b. lovers' names marked in sand
   c. the increased wisdom gained in maturing
   d. the importance of planning ahead.

5. To fit with stanzas 3 and 4, the word "mine" in line 16 must refer to a date longer than the
   a. speaker's lifetime
   b. time between low and high tide
   c. passage of a year
   d. entire night.

6. After asking "What shall I build" the speaker names Troy and Rome as examples of
   a. ridiculous myths
   b. civilizations that did not last
   c. buried cities worth excavating
   d. the birthplaces of his heroes.

7. Lines 19–20 hold a reference to the possibility of gaining
   a. experience traveling
   b. exceptional strength and endurance
   c. extra days of vacation
   d. lasting fame.

8. The speaker's final answer to the question of what to build or write is
   a. a clean life
   b. charm and personality
   c. a name worthy of respect
   d. nothing.

9. "Cities not built to last" are echoes of what words in stanza 5? How does the "unremaining mound" in line 6 carry the same idea as the final stanza?

10. The "confounding main" serves best as a symbol for
    a. destruction caused by the violence of nature
    b. time's turning human works to nothing
    c. hope for a new tomorrow
    d. the swiftness with which happiness can be washed away.

Expressing Your Ideas

Basing your discussion on ideas brought out by the preceding Focusing In section and adding conclusions of your own, write a composition of three to five paragraphs on one of the following topics.

1. Discuss the symbols in "Smooth Between Sea and Land." Explain how the sea, the "confounding main" that sweeps the sandy shore clean of everything, serves as the major symbol.

   Before beginning to write, ask yourself such questions as these:

   > What do the children playing in the sand represent? How does the image of childhood carry through the poem?
   >
   > A *literary allusion*—a reference to literature, history, myth, or the Bible—often serves as a basis for comparison. How does the allusion to Adam strengthen the idea behind the poem?
   >
   > What other comparisons lead to an understanding of the poem?

   You need not specifically answer these questions in your composition, but consider their significance before organizing and writing your paper.

2. "Smooth Between Sea and Land" contains an underlying idea similar to that of "Ozymandias" on page 59. Compare the two poems in a thoughtful, carefully organized composition of three to five paragraphs.

   Before writing, give thought to the similarity in the ideas of the two poems and the difference in their presentation. Were the poets seeking a similar or different effect? Which poem is more personal? Give proof from each poem to support your conclusions.

Variations on a Theme

In music, a theme is a melody that recurs, often with variations. In poetry, a theme is the subject that a poet "plays upon." As in music, a poetic theme may be stated directly or merely suggested. Themes express ideas about life, about human beings' place in the universe, about nature and human nature, about any subject imaginable—taking up questions almost everyone asks and never stops asking.

The theme of a poem may be serious or humorous, trivial or important. And you should not expect a poem to give advice on how to live. But as anyone who reads advice columns knows, there is one subject more people seek and give advice about than any other. In this section you'll read three poems with similar themes: love.

Love me not

Love me not for comely* grace,
For my pleasing eye or face,
Nor for any outward part,
No, nor for my constant heart;
For those may fail or turn to ill,   5
  So thou and I shall sever.*
Keep therefore a true woman's eye,
And love me still, but know not why,
So hast thou the same reason still
  To dote* upon me ever.   10

—Anonymous

1. comely: attractive. **6. sever:** separate. **10. dote:** give attention beyond the usual degree.

THINKING IT THROUGH

Often the key lines in a poem do not come at the beginning. "Love me not" is such an example.

1. Lines 7 and 8 are the key to the poem and provide the advice that the speaker gives. To whom is this advice given? How would you express it in modern English?

2. What three poor reasons for loving are given in lines 1–4?

3. Why does the speaker feel that any of these might cause separation?

4. In line 7, why is the word *true* ambiguous? Why might this be intentional?

5. What does the speaker feel is the advantage for a woman to "love... but know not why"?

Here is another poem on the theme of love and its reasons.

Sonnet 14

If thou must love me, let it be for nought*
Except for love's sake only. Do not say,
"I love her for her smile—her look—her way
Of speaking gently,—for a trick of thought
That falls in well with mine, and certes* brought   5
A sense of pleasant ease on such a day;"
For these things in themselves, beloved, may
Be changed, or change for thee,—and love so wrought*
May be unwrought so. Neither love me for
Thine own dear pity's wiping my cheeks dry: 10
A creature might forget to weep, who bore
Thy comfort long, and lose thy love thereby.
But love me for love's sake, that evermore
Thou may'st love me through love's eternity.

——Elizabeth Barrett Browning

1. nought: nothing. **5. certes:** certainly, in truth. **8. wrought:** attained or brought about (a past tense of the verb *work*.)

THINKING IT THROUGH

1. Where in "Sonnet 14" is the speaker's advice? To whom is it given? How would you express this advice in present-day English?

2. In lines 3–6, what four poor reasons does the speaker give for loving?

3. Why does the speaker feel that these might lead to love being "unwrought"?

4. In lines 9–12, why does the speaker feel that loving someone out of pity might also cause love to be lost?

5. What does the final line give as the result of following the speaker's advice?

Finally, here is another variation on the theme of love.

Warning

To love a man wholly
love him
feet first
   head down
   eyes cold   5
   closed
in depression.

It is too easy to love
a surfer
white eyes   10
godliness &
   bronze
in the bright sun.

———Alice Walker

FOCUSING IN

1. What do you know of the speaker in "Love me not"? What qualities would you use to describe him: caring, faithful, loving, generous, unselfish—or their opposites? Use the poem to support your opinion.

2. How does the speaker in Browning's poem ("Sonnet 14") differ in attitude toward the loved one? What is this speaker's greatest concern?

3. In which of the first two poems is the speaker only concerned with being loved and unconcerned with giving love?

4. How does the speaker's attitude in Alice Walker's poem ("Warning") differ from the attitudes expressed in the other poems?

5. Compare the *you* to whom each of these poems is addressed. How is each different?

6. Alice Walker's word choice contrasts strikingly with that of the other two poets. How would you state her idea in an expanded version?

7. By writing in free verse, Walker carries out the idea of this being a "warning." Considering the fact that it warns against loving a surfer "in the sun," where do you imagine such a warning would be posted?

8. How do the form and diction of Walker's poem carry out this idea?

9. How is Walker's theme similar to Browning's and the anonymous poet's?

10. Which poem do you think conveys its idea more clearly and easily? Which do you believe expresses the most feeling? Be prepared to support your ideas with effective reasons.

Feeling the Rhythm

Rhythm is a natural part of life. There is rhythm to your heartbeat, to your footsteps, to the ticking of a clock, even to your conversation. What other rhythms can you name that people sometimes take for granted?

You can feel the beat of music without having a technical grasp of tempo. So, too you can feel the rhythm of poetry without knowing much about meter. But by noting a poet's use of regular rhythm, you can better understand its effect.

EXPERIMENTING WITH WORDS AND IDEAS

Poetic rhythm, whether regular or free, begins in everyday speech. As an illustration, try saying the following words as a robot might speak them.

> Our ship has come to offer you a journey into boundless
> space.

Electronic voices utter words in a monotone, giving every syllable equal weight. Now read the same sentence in an ordinary voice, and listen to the differences.

Poetic rhythm is based on the rhythms of actual speech:

1. People give emphasis to certain words, often nouns and verbs, in order to call attention to their importance.

2. In words of two or more syllables, one syllable almost always receives more stress. What multisyllabic words does the robot's sentence include? Where does the stress fall in each?

   Mark the stresses in the following words: return, consider, understand, personal, outlandish, traveling, adjustable, consideration, suspend.

3. The alternation of stressed and unstressed syllables makes it easier to extract meaning. Both everyday speech and poetry require rhythm. Poetry, however, uses more consistent, regular rhythm.

Poetic Scansion

Our ship has come to offer you a journey into boundless
space.

While reading the robot's words aloud, perhaps you found yourself caught up in the beat of its regular rhythm. In fact, you'd find the sentence easier to say if it were written in two even lines:

Our ship has come to offer you

A journey into boundless space.

Beginning with the two-syllable words, mark, or scan, each accented syllable, for example, óffer. Next, mark each one-syllable word that deserves emphasis. The result should look like this:

Our shíp has cóme to óffer yóu

A jóurney ínto bóundless spáce.

Unstressed syllables are also marked. Fully marked, the lines will look like this:

Our shíp has cóme to óffer yóu

A jóurney ínto bóundless spáce.

The result? A regular pattern of stressed and unstressed syllables, repeated four times. Each unit of the pattern is called a *foot*. This one, called an *iamb* (⏑ ′), is the most common foot in English poetry because it most closely follows the rhythm of everyday speech. When a poem has lines of equal length and a regular rhythm, check first to see if it's *iambic*. Chances are good you'll be right.

The number of feet per line can also be noted. Each combination has a special term, shown in the following examples.

1. Nŏ gáin,
   nŏ páin.   (one iambic foot per line = iambic monometer)

2. Dŏ yoú | bĕlíeve
   ĭt's tíme | tŏ leáve?   (two iambic feet per line = iambic dimeter)

3. Ĭ něv|ĕr sáw | ă moór,
   Ĭ něv|ĕr sáw | thĕ séa   (three iambic feet per line = iambic trimeter)

4. Fŏr thóse | măy fáil | ŏr túrn | tŏ íll
   Ănd lóve | mĕ stíll, | bŭt knów | nŏt whý
   (four iambic feet per line = iambic tetrameter)

5. Ĭf thóu | mŭst lóve | mĕ, lét | ĭt bé | fŏr nóught
   Ĕxcépt | fŏr lóve's | săke ón|ly̆. Dó | nŏt sáy
   (five iambic feet per line = iambic pentameter)

Note that most poetic feet are made up of one stressed syllable and one or more unstressed syllables (an exception is the spondee: ′ ′). Vertical lines are used to separate feet.

Experimenting with Words and Ideas

All but two of the following examples are written in iambic feet. Copy the lines on a separate sheet of paper. Then mark the syllables and label the *meter*—the type and number of feet used in the verse. If an example is not iambic, try to determine its pattern of stressed and unstressed syllables. Other possibilities are anapest (˘ ˘ ′), trochee (′ ˘), and dactyl (′ ˘ ˘). When scanning a poem, do so one line at a time.

1. Though nature made him kind,
   Misfortune made him cruel.

2. You please me more
   Than words can say.

3. Oft have I seen at some cathedral door . . .

4. What a chubby baby that is!

5. He came to ask what he had found,
   That was so large, and smooth, and round.

6. Pretend,
   my friend,
   to lend,
   an ear.

7. Easily, merrily Ted tapped the tympani.

8. "My name is Ozymandias, King of Kings:
   Look on my works, ye Mighty, and despair!"

Here Comes Shakespeare

Iambic pentameter is the meter most frequently associated with William Shakespeare. The majority of his plays, from *Romeo and Juliet* to *A Winter's Tale,* were written in this meter.

A poetic form, the Shakespearean sonnet bears his name. English has other sonnet forms (poems of fourteen lines written in iambic pentameter), but Shakespeare's rhyme scheme provides a special way of expressing his themes.

Sonnet 29

When in disgrace with fortune and men's eyes
I all alone beweep my outcast state,
And trouble deaf heaven with my bootless* cries,
And look upon myself, and curse my fate;
Wishing me like to one more rich in hope,   5
Featured like him, like him with friends possessed,
Desiring this man's art, and that man's scope,*
With what I most enjoy contented least;
Yet in these thoughts myself almost despising,
Haply* I think on thee—and then my state,   10
Like to the lark at break of day arising
From sullen earth, sings hymns at heaven's gate;
  For thy sweet love remembered, such wealth brings
  That then I scorn* to change my state with kings.

——William Shakespeare

3. **bootless:** useless. 7. **scope:** opportunity or room for action or influence. **10. Haply:** by chance, by luck. **14. scorn:** reject with scorn.

THINKING IT THROUGH

The key to "Sonnet 29" lies in the last two lines, a rhymed couplet. Think these two lines through before considering how the rest of the poem leads to this conclusion.

1. What words in line 13 mean the same as "such wealth"?

2. Aware of having "such wealth," how does the speaker feel about his situation or place in life? Compare this final couplet with the first twelve lines.

3. In the first four lines, what is the speaker's situation? What does he lack that is desirable to him?

4. What are three ways that he responds to this state?

5. In lines 5–7, what five things does the speaker envy in others?

6. What feelings does the speaker express toward himself?

7. In lines 10–12, what change comes over the speaker? Why?

8. What information is given about the one called *thee* in this sonnet?

9. Why is no further identification of *thee* given? Would the sonnet gain or lose if more were known? Explain your answer.

Watching a Mind at Play

What ideas do you associate with a bat? You may think of a furry, mouselike animal with wings. It is active at night and usually sleeps by day. Many bats navigate by sending out short, high-frequency sounds—a kind of animal radar. Roughly, that's what a bat is like.

But how is a bat like the human mind? In the poem on the next page, Richard Wilbur asks you to explore this theme. Wilbur's poem is mainly in iambic pentameter, the same meter used by William Shakespeare over four hundred years ago.

Mind

Mind in its purest play is like some bat
That beats about in caverns all alone,
Contriving* by a kind of senseless wit
Not to conclude against a wall of stone.

It has no need to falter or explore;   5
Darkly it knows what obstacles are there,
And so may weave and flitter, dip and soar
In perfect courses through the blackest air.

And has this simile a like perfection?
The mind is like a bat. Precisely. Save*   10
That in the very happiest intellection
A graceful error may correct the cave.

——Richard Wilbur

3. contriving: inventing, devising, figuring out. **10. save:** except.

FOCUSING IN

Write your answers on a separate sheet of paper.

1. List expressions from lines 3 and 11 that rename, clarify, and expand on the sense in which Wilbur uses the word *mind*.

2. List three words that echo the sense of "purest."

3. The phrase "in its purest play" implies a mind
   a. attempting to solve a difficulty
   b. trapped in an inescapable situation
   c. engaged in flights of fancy
   d. fallen victim to its own foolishness.

4. The poem compares the mind "in play" to a bat in a cavern. Thus, the word *beats* refers to the beating of the bat's
   a. heart
   b. wings
   c. enemies
   d. head against the wall.

5. What are two difficulties named in stanza 2 that might prevent a creature other than a bat from soaring without danger "in perfect courses"?

6. In stanza 2, the radarlike abilities of the bat are best expressed by what phrase?

7. The word *conclude* has a double meaning in reference to the mind and the bat. Explain each.

8. The word *senseless* implies that the bat/mind misses the obstacles
   a. because of its stupidity
   b. through lack of feeling
   c. without conscious effort
   d. through sheer luck.

9. The words "weave and flitter, dip and soar" carry the connotation of the bat/mind
   a. acting lost and confused
   b. being in constant danger
   c. seeking an exit from the cave
   d. having playful fun.

10. The phrase "darkly it knows" echoes and adds to the phrase
    a. senseless wit
    b. purest play
    c. wall of stone
    d. all alone.

11. Line 9 asks, ". . . has this simile a like perfection?" What is being compared to what?

12. The word *happiest* in line 11 serves as an echo of what word in the first stanza, naming the kind of activity the bat/mind is engaged in?

13. Since the bat stands for the human mind, the cave most likely stands for
    a. the human skull
    b. perplexing problems and ideas
    c. the world and surrounding universe
    d. the enemies of rational thought.
       Before choosing, consider the following:
       How does the fact that the bat can "dip and soar" affect the idea of the cave as a metaphor for the skull?
       What further proof comes from the fact that *mind* is singular and *caverns* in line 2 is plural?

14. Based on your answers to the foregoing, explain the last line, including the ideas behind the words "graceful error" and "correct."

Choosing from What You Know

A la carte means ordering a meal from a menu that prices each item separately.
What "dishes" are being offered in Kenneth Fearing's poem? What kind of
"restaurant" would have such a menu?

A La Carte

Some take to liquor, some turn to prayer,
Many prefer to dance, others to gamble, and a few
resort to* gas or the gun.
(Some are lucky, and some are not.)

Name your choice, any selection from one to twenty-five: 5
Music from Harlem? A Viennese waltz on the slot-machine
   phonograph at Jack's Bar & Grill? Or a Brahms
    Concerto over WXV?*
(Many like it wild, others sweet.)

Champagne for supper, murder for breakfast, romance for lunch   10
and terror for tea,
This is not the first time nor will it be the last time
   the world has gone to hell.
(Some can take it, and some cannot.)

                ——Kenneth Fearing

---

3. resort to: seek an escape through. **8. WXV:** radio station.

THINKING IT THROUGH

1. Lines 1–3 list five different escapes that people turn to. What does each term represent?

2. According to the poem, what determines whether someone makes a good or bad choice?

3. Lines 6–9 list a variety of music. What does each choice represent?

4. In addition to music, what else can the pronoun *it* stand for in line 9?

5. Lines 10–11 clearly bring out the idea that this poem is about a type of menu. What in life does each of the following represent: champagne, murder, romance, terror?

6. What word in line 13 names the "restaurant" that the poem's *a la carte* listings come from?

7. This poem was written in 1940. Was the world "overtaken by evil" at that time? Explain the reasons for your answer.

8. Is the poem really trying to prove the "world has gone to hell" or the opposite? Support your answer.

9. In the final line, what is "it" that some people can take and some can't?

10. Does this poem represent the world as it is today? What, if any, changes are needed to bring the poem up-to-date?

On Your Own

What joys can people find in writing and reading poetry? After reading the poem on the following page, write your ideas in your poetry notebook.

The Secret

Two girls discover
the secret of life
in a sudden line of
poetry.

I who don't know the
secret wrote
the line. They told me

(Through a third person)
they had found it
but not what it was
not even

what line it was. No doubt
by now, more than a week
later, they have forgotten
the secret,

the line, the name of
the poem. I love them
for finding what
I can't find,

and for loving me
for the line I wrote,
and for forgetting it
so that

a thousand times, till death
finds them, they may
discover it again, in other
lines

in other
happenings. And for
wanting to know it,
for

assuming there is
such a secret, yes,
for that
most of all

—Denise Levertov

Expressing Yourself

Get into the swing! In order to break the rules with intelligence, it's helpful to know what the rules are.

That's one of the secrets of success of poets like Denise Levertov.

In many ways free verse takes more discipline than poetry with traditional rhyme and rhythm. That's because free verse requires self-discipline, with the poet responsible for making the decisions about how to express the theme best. There's no set meter, form, or rhyming words to follow.

Discover how it feels to work with rhyme and rhythm.

Write a rhymed couplet (more if you prefer) in each of the following meters:

1. iambic trimeter

2. iambic tetrameter

3. iambic pentameter

Choose as your topic an emotion, a color, an idea such as success or ambition. You can even choose something silly.

The purpose of this exercise is to give you the feel of writing in different rhythms and seeking a rhyme for the end of each line.

When you have written your sample couplets, try to compose a more serious poem, at least a quatrain in length, that grows from your practice attempts.

Summing Up

Where to begin analyzing a poem? Work from what you know.

Find a key line or an idea.

Don't try to absorb the entire poem all at once. Break it into manageable units—a sentence, a phrase—even figuring out the use of a single word can start you on the way.

Don't let yourself be put off by long, involved sentences—or even by lack of punctuation. Be your own editor, and think the sentences through so they read clearly.

Don't feel you must begin at the beginning and work out each detail, step-by-step, as you go. Often, the end of a poem contains important clues to help you explain the first line or stanza.

Feel free to skim through the poem quickly, then skip around and move back and forth—so you know your way around.

A poem is not a map that directs you to find the shortest way to the end. It's closer to a globe, made up of interlocking pieces, that leads you to understand the relationship of each part to the whole.

Don't be afraid to ask why each piece is necessary. Don't expect to know everything at once or even to find answers to every detail.

Using what you know to discover what you don't know is the process called thinking and learning by doing.

CHAPTER TEN

Sharpening Your Skills

uch of your time in school is spent developing skills; soon these become second nature. And so it should be with time spent studying poetry.

Poetry is not a science. It doesn't lend itself to mechanical checklists and formulas. As you've seen by Focusing In, some ideas and details in poems lend themselves to factual, direct answers. But just as many allow a variety of interpretations.

A good reader needs the ability to know how much can be said with certainty about a poem. It's also necessary to determine associated ideas, relationships, and figurative meanings that fulfill the conditions set forth in a poem. And to realize when a reader's imagination has run so far astray that the poem itself gets left behind.

The skills you've gained in reading poetry are yours to rely on. Used consciously or not, they will help you find the basic thread that ties a poem together and makes it a unified whole.

Each poem in this chapter presents a special difficulty and, it's hoped, a special reward. Each builds on skills mastered in earlier chapters. So each poem offers a chance to sharpen your skills, and an opportunity to continue growing.

Lyric or Narrative?

The following poem by Walter de la Mare appeals to people's natural love of storytelling, just as folk and literary ballads do. Yet this poem, ''Autumn,'' includes almost no clues about what actually happened.

Although the circumstances are left untold, the poem reveals their significance through the speaker's comparison of the current autumn to the season past. The changes that have come with the changing season represent the change that came into the speaker's life. And, by comparing these differences, you become aware of the meaningfulness of what happened, even though no background details are given.

"Autumn" is an example of a poem that requires close and careful reading. Then it practically invites you to invent details that account for the feelings it expresses.

Autumn

There is a wind where the rose was;
Cold rain where sweet grass was;
  And clouds like sheep
  Stream o'er the steep
Grey skies where the lark was.   5

Nought gold where your hair was;
Nought warm where your hand was;
  But phantom, forlorn,
  Beneath the thorn,
Your ghost where your face was.   10

Sad winds where your voice was;
Tears, tears where my heart was;
  And ever with me,
  Child, ever with me,
Silence where hope was.   15

——Walter de la Mare

FOCUSING IN

Write your answers on a separate sheet of paper.

1. In stanza 1, what three good things are now gone?

2. What three things have replaced each?

3. In line 4, the word *steep* describing skies carries the metaphorical effect of
   a. being too expensive
   b. going straight up
   c. being quick and unexpected
   d. being difficult to surmount or overcome

4. Taken with the rest of the poem, *lark* in line 5 becomes a symbol of
   a. mourning
   b. happiness
   c. forgetfulness
   d. the future.

5. In stanza 2, what three physical things does the speaker miss?

6. In line 7, the poet writes that there is now "nought," or nothing, "warm." How is this line parallel to line 2?

7. What two words in lines 8–10 reveal why the speaker feels so alone and forlorn? What is their significance?

8. What word in stanza 3 specifically addresses the *you* in the poem?

9. In stanza 3, what good things in the speaker's life are gone?

10. What has replaced these three things?

THINKING IT THROUGH

Relate your ideas to the poem, allowing room for individual interpretations that fit the conditions set forth in the poem.

1. In this poem, the specific experience is less important than the speaker's response. What must have happened to cause the speaker to have such deep feelings?

2. How much do you know about the other person involved? Is it necessary that the person be a young child? What range of ages fit the circumstances?

3. Is the poem really about autumn, or is it actually an "autumn of the spirit"? Or both? Use the poem to support your opinion.

4. What situation might justify someone's feeling as the speaker does?

Expressing Your Ideas

Create a fictional situation that accounts for the feelings that the speaker expresses in the poem "Autumn." Then adopt the speaker's persona and write a letter to an imaginary friend or relative, explaining the loss and how you would feel if you were forced to face it.

Every Detail Counts

"Childhood rememberances are always a drag." How much can you tell or guess about the speaker of the following poem, just from the opening line?

In "Nikki-Roasa," the speaker's name is the same as the poet's. Yet even that fact shouldn't cause you to break the habit of thinking of the speaker as a persona created by the poet to give shape to an idea.

As you read, consider: Why didn't Giovanni choose to follow standard rules of punctuation and capitalization? Although the poem is told in first person, why does the poet delay having Nikki-Roasa call herself *I* until line 24? How and why does the poem have meaning that goes beyond a single, autobiographical view?

Nikki-Roasa

childhood rememberances are always a drag
if you're Black
you always remember things like living in Woodlawn
with no inside toilet
and if you become famous or something   5
they never talk about how happy you were to have your mother
all to yourself and
how good the water felt when you got your bath from one of those
big tubs that folk in chicago barbecue in
and somehow when you talk about home   10
it never gets across how much you
understood their feelings
as the whole family attended meetings about Hollydale
and even though you remember
your biographers never understand   15
your father's pain as he sells his stock
and another dream goes
and though you're poor it isn't poverty that
concerns you
and though they fought a lot   20
it isn't your father's drinking that makes any difference
but only that everybody is together and you
and your sister have happy birthdays and very good christ-
masses and I really hope no white person ever has cause to
write about me because they never understand Black love   25
is Black wealth and they'll probably talk about my hard
childhood and never understand that all the while I was
quite happy

——Nikki Giovanni

THINKING IT THROUGH

1. Is the speaker's voice that of a child or of an adult? How does Giovanni's choice and use of words create this impression?

2. Judging from lines 3–10, who is meant by *you*?

3. What choices has the poet made concerning capitalization? What effect does she create as a result?

4. In lines 1–10, what two facts are given about the kind of home Nikki-Roasa lived in?

5. Even though nothing specific is said about Woodlawn, what kind of neighborhood must it be, considering Nikki-Roasa's home there?

6. What good things about Nikki-Roasa's childhood are brought out in the first ten lines?

7. In line 12, the poet writes of understanding ''their feelings.'' Who is ''their?'' Even without knowing what Hollydale is, what important detail do you learn from lines 12–13 about her family?

8. Using line 15 as the key, who might *they* be in line 6? Who else could *they* stand for?

9. In lines 18–21, what three negative things does the speaker reveal about her family life? Why are these best told now rather than earlier?

10. What words express the speaker's feelings about the importance of these things?

11. What are three things the speaker says do matter?

12. Are these things important to all children? If so, why does the speaker say white people won't understand?

13. Why would biographers of famous people like to ''talk about'' hard childhoods? Would this be true of any famous person? Give reasons for your response.

14. The last line states ''all the while I was quite happy.'' What word in line 25 explains the reason for that happiness?

15. What effects does the poet achieve by using the word *you* instead of *I* or *she* in reference to Nikki-Roasa?

Expressing Yourself

Write a portrait of yourself or of someone you know. Try to include details and descriptive clues that will make your reader see and share an understanding of this person.

Do not try to include everything, but select one or two traits that are a distinctive part of this person's character and try to present them in a clear, revealing light. Your goal is not to *tell* your reader what to think but to *show* the person, both as an individual and as someone to whom everyone can relate.

You may choose a poetic technique or write your portrait in prose.

Taking Sides

As you read about the following couple, don't forget that the story is told exclusively from one person's point of view. Who's right? Who's wrong? Does the poet want you to take the situation seriously? Is the poem making fun of the speaker? Of the woman? Of both?

Before you decide, look for traits that bring the characters to life. Know what happened and why. The first line describes the woman as speaking bitterly. What tone does the speaker use?

Here's a poem that seems to invite an argument among its readers about who's wrong and who's right. If you want to choose sides, be sure to draw valid conclusions from the poem to support your ideas.

Intimates

Don't you care for my love? she said bitterly.

I handed her the mirror, and said:
Please address these questions to the proper person!
Please make all requests to head-quarters!
In all matters of emotional importance   5
please approach the supreme authority direct!—
So I handed her the mirror.

And she would have broken it over my head,
but she caught sight of her own reflection
and that held her spellbound for two seconds   10
while I fled.

—D. H. Lawrence

Intimates: close friends or associates, especially those who confide in one another.

THINKING IT THROUGH

1. Concerning line 3, what question does the speaker suggest the woman ask the mirror?

2. Why would he call the mirror and its reflection "head-quarters"?

3. If the woman questioned the mirror, what are two possibilities for who *you* might be?

4. What must the speaker believe the woman cares most about? What does he imply about the mirror's response?

5. In the first four lines, what two clues reveal that this is part of an ongoing argument?

6. What is the intended tone of the words "supreme authority" in line 6? By denying involvement in matters of "emotional importance," what does the speaker reveal about their real relationship as "intimates"?

7. What effect does the poet create by having the speaker repeat the word *please* at the beginning of three lines?

8. Give at least two reasons for the man's handing the woman the mirror.

9. Does the poem take a serious or humorous approach to its subject? Give reasons for your conclusion.

10. What does the poem reveal as the chief character traits of the woman? Is her character exaggerated or true to life? Do you think the poet created her as a stereotype of most women? Why do you feel as you do?

11. Who behaved the worse toward the other, the man or the woman? Support your opinion.

12. As a verb, *intimate* (in/ ə māt) means "to make known indirectly, suggest." How does the double meaning apply to this poem?

Playing Mind Games

In the following poem, Randall Jarrell speaks through the persona of a sick child, using dialogue that takes place only in the child's inventive mind. It may be a challenge to follow the imagined conversation and to keep track of who speaks.

As you enter the child's world of make-believe, remember to ask yourself why the poet has chosen this form and technique. Decide his purpose in portraying the thoughts of a child who asks more than imagination can give.

A Sick Child

The postman comes when I am still in bed.
"Postman, what do you have for me today?"
I say to him. (But really I'm in bed.)
Then he says—what shall I have him say?

"This letter says that you are president   5
Of—this word here; it's a republic."
Tell them I can't answer right away.
"It's your duty." No, I'd rather just be sick.

Then he tells me there are letters saying everything
That I can think of that I want for them to say.   10
I say, "Well, thank you very much. Good-bye."
He is ashamed, and turns and walks away.

If I can think of it, it isn't what I want.
I want. . .I want a ship from some near star
To land in the yard, and beings to come out   15
And think to me: "So this is where you are!
Come." Except that they won't do,
I thought of them. . .And yet somewhere there must be
Something that's different from everything.
All that I've never thought of—think of me!   20

—Randall Jarrell

THINKING IT THROUGH

Work in pairs on the following questions, which lend themselves to agreement.

1. All of the action in this poem takes place in a child's imagination. Where is the child, and why does he or she have time for thinking?

2. What does the child imagine saying, and what does he or she imagine is said by others?

3. Rewrite stanzas 2 and 3 so they are stated in dialogue. Try to decide on two advantages of Jarrell's using a combination of direct and indirect quotations.

4. The imaginary postman says, "...president/Of—this word here; it's a republic." In keeping with the conditions of the poem, why couldn't he pronounce the word or even name a republic?

5. Why would the postman feel ashamed as a result of the child's response to getting letters "saying everything...I want for them to say"?

6. How does line 13 explain the child's rejection of the presidency and attitude toward all the other ideas?

7. How is the space ship like the letters, and why does the child say, "they won't do"?

8. What would be the advantage of having "something that's different" think of the child first? Would this be possible or impossible? Explain.

EXPERIMENTING WITH WORDS AND IDEAS

Share your ideas about the following questions, which allow a variety of viewpoints and opinions.

1. What really was the child's problem: boredom brought on by being sick; an excess of imagination; or something else? Be prepared to justify your opinion.

2. Is the child typical of or different from most children? Explain. Do you think others feel the same as the child most of the time, part of the time, once in a while, or never?

3. Can you think of a time when you or someone you know expressed similar feelings? What was the incident?

4. In the last line, the child calls on "All that I've never thought of..." Why isn't the child looking in the right place for help? What, if anything, will help?

5. Reread "A Sick Child" after your discussions, and note new dimensions to your understanding that result from sharing others' viewpoints.

On Your Own

The following poem practically begs you to put yourself in the picture and take sides about its accuracy. Write your reactions in your poetry notebook.

The Adversary

A mother's hardest to forgive.
Life is the fruit she longs to hand you,
Ripe on a plate. And while you live,
Relentlessly* she understands you.

—Phyllis McGinley

Adversary: an opponent. **4. relentlessly:** unyieldingly, steadily, not giving up.

Questions Without Answers

Not every question requires or even expects an answer. And it's often helpful to decide why a question is being asked. Is it meant to start you thinking? To rouse you to argument? To lead you to a specific conclusion? To make you question the validity of the question itself?

William Stafford uses a question as the title of the following poem—"What If We Were Alone?" Who are "we"...and where are "we"? There's no way to answer, unless you read on.

What if there weren't any stars? But there are, and it's impossible to imagine a universe without them. As you read the following poem, you'll discover how Stafford builds to a conclusion that is based on traceable logic and is reached by posing questions beyond most human beings' ability to grasp.

What If We Were Alone?

What if there weren't any stars?
What if only the sun and the earth
circled alone in the sky? What if
no one ever found anything outside
this world right here?—no Galileo*   5
could say, "Look—it is out there,
a hint of whether we are everything."

Look out at the stars. Yes—cold
space. Yes, we are so distant that
the mind goes hollow to think it.   10
But something is out there. Whatever
our limits, we are led outward. We glimpse
company. Each glittering point of light
beckons: "There is something beyond."

The moon rolls through the trees, rises   15
from them, and waits. In the river all
night a voice floats from rock
to sandbar, to log. What kind of listening
can follow quietly enough? We bow, and
the voice that falls through the rapids   20
calls all the rocks by their secret names.

————William Stafford

5. **Galileo:** Italian astronomer, 1564–1642.

T H I N K I N G   I T   T H R O U G H

1. The questions in lines 1–5 provide answers to questions raised by the title: Whom does the poet refer to as *we*? What is the place referred to, where we might be alone? Support your conclusions.

2. By turning his telescope toward the skies, the astronomer Galileo saw countless stars invisible to the human eye and provided evidence to support theories unproven before then. Why does the poet have Galileo say, "Look—it is out there"?

3. Stafford calls *it* "a hint of whether we are everything." In the terms of the poem, what would being "everything" mean? Why did Galileo's discovery provide nothing more solid than a hint?

4. How does stanza 2 echo the words of Galileo? How does this direction to "Look..." express a different idea?

5. In lines 8–10, Stafford uses three adjectives to describe a person's relationship to space. Identify them, and explain why each is appropriate.

6. Instead of questions, lines 11–14 present four factual statements about people's feelings toward outer space. What are they? Why does the poem prepare you to accept them as valid?

7. What words in lines 11–14 lead you to believe that the poem refers to more than people's interest in the science of astronomy, the discovery of new galaxies, and the exploration of space? What might this interest be?

8. How do lines 15 and 16 link the last stanza with the first two stanzas? How is the reader's attention refocused?

9. How is the moon personified? Why is the moon's personification in keeping with stanza 2? How does it prepare you for lines to come?

10. Although the last stanza contains only one direct question, what other questions does it raise? Why doesn't the poem attempt to answer them?

11. What makes the voice heard in the river seem mysterious? What attitude does the listener take toward it? What words direct you to give this answer?

12. After considering the entire poem, what answer are you apparently expected to give to the title question, "What if we were alone?" Why?

A Different Observation About Space

Even though two poems apparently have the same topic, the good reader addresses each on its own terms and follows where the poet leads—always ready for a few surprises!

Norman MacCaig's "Stars and Planets" unfolds in a direction almost exactly opposite from William Stafford's poem and makes a far different observation. But understanding both requires you to exercise the same skills—close attention to the poet's preciseness of description, awareness of personification and figurative language, and a willingness to go beyond the face value to discover the underlying theme.

Stars and Planets

Trees are cages for them: water holds its breath
To balance them without smudging on its delicate meniscus,*
Children watch them playing in their heavenly playground;
Men use them to lug* ships across oceans, through firths.*

They seem so twinkle-still, but they never cease   5
Inventing new spaces and huge explosions
And migrating in mathematical tribes over
The steppes* of space at their outrageous ease.

It's hard to think that the earth is one—
This poor sad bearer of wars and disasters   10
Rolls-Roycing round the sun with its load of gangsters,
Attended only by the loveless moon.

——Norman MacCaig

2. **meniscus:** *upper* surface of a liquid. 4. **lug:** drag or haul with difficulty. **firths:** narrow inlets of the sea. 8. **steppes:** vast, level, treeless areas of land.

FOCUSING IN

Write your answers on a separate sheet of paper.

1. In stanza 1 of "Stars and Planets," *them* means
   a. birds and leaves
   b. stars and planets
   c. ships and planes
   d. light and shadows.

2. The metaphor *cages* calls to mind how trees
   a. act as homes for birds' nests
   b. create shadows that block out light
   c. are material for construction
   d. have crisscrossing branches through which stars peek.

3. The poet wants you to picture the water as
   a. tense about the reflection of stars on its surface
   b. afraid of a falling star's crashing into it
   c. smudged with the shadows of dark clouds
   d. holding its breath because of the strong wind.

4. In line 3, MacCaig
   a. introduces children playing in the pond
   b. shows the irony of human children doing nothing but watch "them" play
   c. personifies stars as children playing, watched by children
   d. introduces the idea of heaven as the eternal playground after death.

5. In line 4, the word *lug* carries the image of
   a. ships pulled by stars used for navigation
   b. the contrast of human labor with the freedom of the heavens
   c. humans' harnessing natural energy as a source of power
   d. the uselessness of humans' efforts to conquer the universe.

6. In stanza 2, *they* are personified through the use of such words as
   a. twinkle-still
   b. inventing new spaces
   c. huge explosions
   d. outrageous

7. Stanza 2 compares stars and planets to
   a. evil geniuses who want to conquer the universe
   b. numberless tribes who migrate to populate all of outer space
   c. mathematicians who are figuring ways to create more powerful explosions
   d. outraged inhabitants of a space being invaded by humans.

8. A reason for its being "hard to think that the earth is one" would be
   a. its superior civilization
   b. its place in the center of the universe
   c. its possession of an atmosphere
   d. its wars and disasters.

9. The image of earth "Rolls-Roycing round the sun with its load of gangsters" contrasts with "them"
   a. smudging its delicate meniscus
   b. playing in their heavenly playground
   c. experiencing huge explosions
   d. behaving outrageously.

10. The main idea of the poem is that humans
    a. have misused their place in the universe
    b. still have new worlds to explore and conquer
    c. are just one of the tribes migrating in space
    d. need to realize the power of love.

The Short and Long of It

Just because a poem is short, it is not necessarily simple and easy to understand. Nor, because it is long, should you expect it to be difficult and complex.

The poems by Emily Dickinson and Walt Whitman on the following pages are very different in length. Yet both are examples of careful development and composition. You'll find every element is a meaningful part of each poem as you discover its key.

In "It dropped so low" by Emily Dickinson, the first question you'll probably ask is, "What is *it*?" But it's a question you shouldn't attempt to answer until the end of the poem. First, discover what happens and why.

The story behind the poem that follows can be told very simply: Something hit the ground and broke into pieces. Instead of getting mad at fate for what happened, the speaker accepts all the blame.

There must be more to it than that! And, of course, there is. Dickinson is a poet who takes advantage of the multiple shades and meanings of words. As you read, try to extract their full value. Look for relationships that direct you to the following poem's figurative meaning and make the act of good reading an act of discovery.

It dropped so low

It dropped so low in my regard*
I heard it hit the ground
And go to pieces on the stones
At bottom of my mind;

Yet blamed the fate that fractured less   5
Than I reviled* myself
For entertaining plated* wares
Upon my silver shelf.

———Emily Dickinson

1. **regard:** opinion, judgment. **6. reviled:** spoke harshly and blamefully. **7. plated:** coated to look like the real thing, not of pure metal.

THINKING IT THROUGH

1. *Stone* is a hard substance, a rock. Which of the following can best be compared with "stones at bottom of my mind"—opinions, likes and dislikes, beliefs, wishes, facts, something different?

2. Compare the ideas expressed by the following: a thought coming off the top of your head, in the middle of your daily concerns, or at the bottom of your mind. What different levels of thought do they describe?

3. What words in line 1 of "It dropped so low" prove that *it* is not an actual object?

4. To *hear* is to notice, to become aware of, to perceive by the ear. How does this definition of *hear* echo the word *regard*?

5. *Ground* includes such meanings as firm, dry land; foundation; support for your position. How do these definitions of *ground* help clarify the answer to question 1?

6. Because it went "to pieces," what fact do you know about "it" in its sense as a metaphor?

7. *Fate* refers to something that is bound to happen or be. What is contradictory about "fate that fractured"? What would be an advantage of blaming fate? What did the speaker do instead?

8. *Wares* may be objects for sale, but can also be talents, abilities, and personal accomplishments. What does the speaker mean by saying that "plated" articles were on the shelf meant for silver? Because of the first stanza, the word *shelf* must also be taken as a metaphor. Explain its figurative sense.

9. The word *entertain* can have these meanings: to admit into or hold in the mind; to exercise hospitality; to hold someone's attention. Discuss how each of these definitions fits the poem, either on a literal or figurative level.

10. "Something I thought highly of proved a fake." Does this statement adequately express the idea that inspired the poem? Explain why or why not.

11. What kinds of things or situations would you nominate as being possible examples of *it*? Compare your ideas with those of your classmates and with the poem to see which qualify and why.

Just as Emily Dickinson concentrates great feeling in every word, so Walt Whitman concentrates much meaning into a poem that, at first glance, seems nothing more than a list. Yet each item represents one of the influences that form someone's character at every stage in childhood and continue to affect that person throughout life.

When you begin reading a longer poem such as the following one, look for elements in composition that tie certain portions together and help you divide the poem into more easily managed parts. What creates unity within each stanza? Can you find a pattern to the poet's handling of place and time? What is the relationship between the objects the poet chooses to name? What changes occur as the poem progresses?

As you read, add each element carefully to the next in order to discover where Whitman is taking this child that went forth...and you.

There Was a Child Went Forth

There was a child went forth every day,
And the first object he looked upon, that object he became,
And that object became part of him for the day or a certain part of the
    day,
Or for many years or stretching cycles of years.

The early lilacs became part of this child   5
And grass and white and red morning-glories, and white and red clover,
    and the song of the phoebe-bird,*
And the Third-month lambs and the sow's pink-faint litter, and the mare's
    foal and the cow's calf,
And the noisy brood of the barnyard or by the mire of the pond-side,
And the fish suspending themselves so curiously below there, and the
    beautiful curious liquid,
And the water-plants with their graceful flat heads, all became part of him10
The field-sprouts of Fourth-month and Fifth-month became part of him,
Winter-grain sprouts and those of the light-yellow corn, and the
    esucculent* roots of the garden,
And the apple-trees covered with blossoms and the fruit afterward, and
    wood-berries, and the commonest weeds by the road.
And the old drunkard staggering home from the outhouse of the tavern
    whence he had lately risen,
And the schoolmistress that passed on her way to the school,   15
And the friendly boys that passed, and the quarrelsome boys,
And the tidy and fresh-cheeked girls, and the barefoot negro boy and girl,
And all the changes of city and country wherever he went.

His own parents, he that had fathered him and she that had conceived him
  in her womb and birthed him,
They gave this child more of themselves than that,   20
They gave him afterward every day, they became part of him.

The mother at home quietly placing the dishes on the supper-table,
The mother with mild words, clean her cap and gown, a wholesome odor
  falling off her person and clothes as she walks by.
The father, strong, self-sufficient, manly, mean, angered, unjust,
The blow, the quick loud word, the tight bargain, the crafty lure,   25
The family usages, the language, the company, the furniture, the yearning
  and swelling heart,
Affection that will not be gainsayed,* the sense of what is real, the thought
  if after all it should prove unreal,
The doubts of day-time and the doubts of night-time, the curious whether
  and how,
Whether that which appears so is so, or is it all flashes and specks?
Men and women crowding fast in the streets, if they are not flashes and
  specks what are they?   30
The streets themselves and the facades* of houses, and goods in the
  windows,
Vehicles, teams, the heavy-planked wharves, the huge crossing at the
  ferries,
The village on the highland seen from afar at sunset, the river between,
Shadows, aureola* and mist, the light falling on roofs and gables of white
  and brown two miles off,
The schooner near by sleepily dropping down the tide, the little boat
  slack-towed astern,   35
The hurrying tumbling waves, quick-broken crests, slapping,
The strata of colored clouds, the long bar of maroon-tint away solitary by
  itself, the spread of purity it lies motionless in,
The horizon's edge, the flying sea-crow, the fragrances of salt marsh and
  shore mud,
These became part of that child who went forth every day, and who now
  goes and will always go forth every day.

——Walt Whitman

6. **phoebe-bird:** named in imitation of its song. 12. **esucculent:** full of juice;
juicy. 27. **gainsayed:** denied, contradicted. 31. **facades:** the fronts of buildings.
34. **aureola:** radiance of light and color, like a halo.

FOCUSING IN

1. The first stanza says "a child went forth." Which is more impressionable, a child or an adult? How does an object that a child looks upon become a part of that child?

2. From lines 5–13, select other examples that share the idea of being part of the early years or early childhood. Explain whether a positive or negative attitude is created toward each.

3. In lines 5–13, how does the poem make a progression in time? How might this fit the poet's purpose?

4. Line 13, containing the adverb *afterward,* introduces a new set of objects. How does the poet use these as positive and negative images, and what effect do they create?

5. Explain the meaning of lines 20 and 21. In line 20, what is *that?* Based on the first stanza, what does Whitman mean by "They gave him afterward every day?"

6. Does the poem speak of the parents as a single influence or as having individual and differing influences? Explain fully.

7. What new idea enters the poem in lines 30 and 31? What can account for this?

8. How and why do the examples given in lines 33–39 qualify as "flashes and specks?"

9. How do the examples in these lines (33–39) differ from those in the first part of the poem, before line 30? What might account for this difference?

10. In the last line, what is the significance of the poet's saying the child not only went forth, but also "goes and will always go forth"? In the context of the poem, how does everyone remain a "child" for his or her entire life?

On Your Own

What in your life has made you "the child who now goes forth"? In your notebook, write an essay or poem in which you attempt to crystalize one or a series of sights and impressions that have gone into making the person you are now and that will always be part of you.

A Final Project

Choose two poems you have studied in this book and write a paper comparing the ideas in the poems and the techniques chosen to express them.

Select poems related in theme, such as the following, or choose other poems. To develop the topic fully, your paper should be at least three pages long. See the Index of Titles and Authors at the end of the book for page numbers.

> "Stars and Planets" and "When I Heard the Learn'd Astronomer"
>
> "Autumn" and "The First Snow-Fall"
>
> "The Unexplorer" and "The Road Not Taken"
>
> "It dropped so low" and another poem by Emily Dickinson
>
> "Intimates" and "Sonnet 14" by Elizabeth Barrett Browning

In your composition, consider the form, language, and approach in each poem, and compare the ideas that make up their substance. Discuss why and how each poet approached the theme in a specific way. You may find some ideas on developing your paper after reading Summing Up.

Summing Up

Because of their concentration, poems require an active reader—ready to jump in and take part in the writing/reading process. Now, as you "go forth," you have learned of many different elements that make up the complex creation called poetry.

Are you aware of all you've met? It isn't possible to call your attention to every aspect of every poem, so you've been asked to concentrate on the elements most important to each. Here is some of the variety you've encountered.

- *Approaches to the subject:* First-person narrative, character sketches, poetic fables, and many more

- *Techniques of rhyme, rhythm, and form:* Free verse or traditional stanza forms, serving as a basis for composition that helps guide you to the poem's meaning

- *Use of literary devices:* Figurative language, personification, and appeals to the five senses, chosen to produce a vivid mental image

- *The idea behind the poem:* Stated directly or indirectly...posing unanswerable questions or revealing personal beliefs...looking inward or outward...trying to make sense of the world with humanity's most precious tool: language.

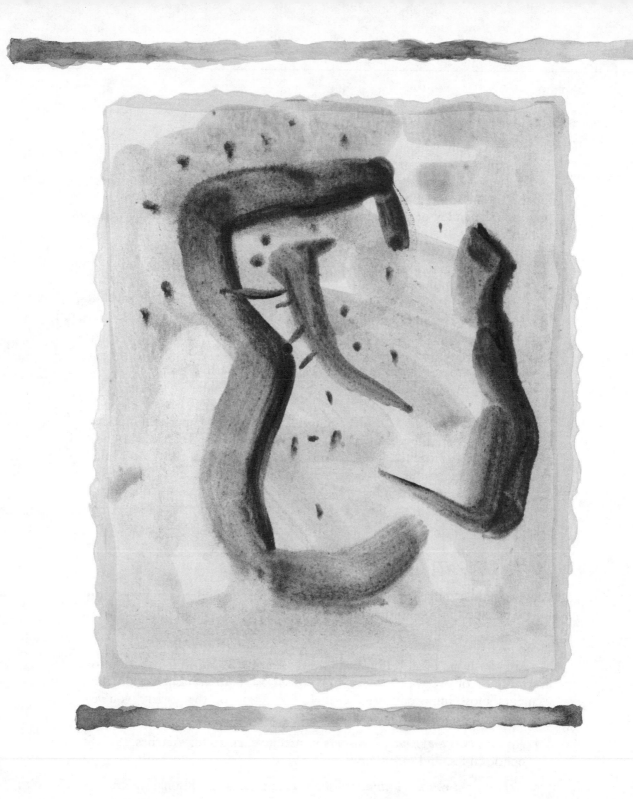

Glossary of Key Literary Terms

Abstract word. A word that names something that can't be identified by the five senses. For example, *justice* and *friendship*.

Active form. "Carl hurled the ball" illustrates the active form of a verb, in which the subject Carl acts instead of being acted upon, in contrast to the passive form, "The ball was hurled by Carl."

Allusion. Reference to a person, place, or event of historical, literary, or mythological importance. In "Smooth Between Sea and Land," A. E. Housman alludes to Eden, Troy and Rome.

Ambiguity. A word or a statement that is capable of being taken in more than one way, with no sure way to determine the intended meaning. "The Constant Lover" by Sir John Suckling has an ambiguous title, since *constant* can mean "faithful and loyal" or "occurring repeatedly."

Anonymous. Created by an unknown person. "Johnie Armstrong" and "Jesse James," like all folk ballads, are anonymous.

Apostrophe. A poem in which an object or idea is addressed as a human being. "Song" by Edmund Waller, which begins, "Go, lovely Rose," is an apostrophe.

Ballad. A poem that tells a story, has qualities of a song, and makes use of rhyme and rhythm. (*See* Folk Ballads and Literary Ballads.)

Cliché. An overworked expression such as "pretty as a picture." Often a simile or metaphor. Acceptable in everyday speech but no longer able to create a fresh or vivid impression.

Coincidence. An odd pairing of events that unexpectedly happen at the same time, apparently by chance.

Coined word. A word invented to suit a current need. *Byte* was coined to name a unit of information for processing in computers.

Composition. The act of "putting together"; bringing separate elements together so that each contributes smoothly to a total effect.

Concrete word. A word that names something that can be perceived by the senses, such as *rock, fortress, wind,* and *shadow*.

Connotation. The associated ideas and feelings a word carries in addition to its denotation or dictionary definition. Although *daring* and *reckless* have similar meanings, their connotations express different attitudes toward the quality they describe.

Couplet. Two lines of poetry of equal length that usually rhyme and that can be complete in themselves or form a part of a longer poem.

> Great things are done when Men & Mountains meet
> This is not done by Jostling in the Street.
> ——William Blake

Denotation. The basic meaning of a word, as shown by the dictionary definition.

Dialect. Words spelled to sound as they do when given a pronunciation peculiar to a certain locality. Examples: *goin'* for *going; Whadda yuh kno'?* for *What do you know?* "Danny Deever" by Rudyard Kipling is a ballad written in the dialect of British soldiers.

Dialogue. Conversation recorded in writing in a poem, play, or story. Dialogue may be set off by quotation marks, as in "Danny Deever," or determined in other ways, such as the pattern of questions and answers in "O What Is That Sound?" by W. H. Auden.

Diction. Choice of words, especially for literary effect.

Direct address. The use of a noun to indicate to whom a speaker is talking. When Johnie Armstrong says, "Fight on, my merry men all," he is addressing his men. Another example is "O where hae ye been, Lord Randal, my son?" addressed to Lord Randal by his mother.

Dirge. A formal song of grief and mourning. Also, a term that identifies a poem with qualities of this type of song, such as "Dirge" by Percy Bysshe Shelley.

Fable. An approach to storytelling that uses fantasy as way to represent a truth. Fables often use animal characters and personification to reveal human traits. "The Flower" by Alfred, Lord Tennyson and "Fable" by Stephen Crane are two examples.

Figurative. The opposite of literal. The term *figurative* applies to something meant to serve as a comparison to something else, not to be taken at its face value.

Folk ballad. A song originally passed from person to person by word of mouth, and therefore anonymous. "Johnie Armstrong,"

"Lord Randal," and "Jesse James" are folk ballads.

Foot. See *Poetic foot*.

Foreshadow. To offer clues about how a plot will develop. In the opening stanza of "The Highwayman," Alfred Noyes foreshadows the ending of the poem when he describes the "ghostly" look of the night sky.

Form. The structure, arrangement, or style of a literary work. It can range from a fixed form, like the sonnet, to one originated by the poet.

Free verse. Poetry that has no fixed pattern. "Nobody loses all the time" by E. E. Cummings and "The Bare Tree" by William Carlos Williams are examples of free verse.

Idyll. A short poem describing a simple and appealing episode or incident. "An Idle Idyll by a very Humble Member of the Great and Noble London Mob" by James Thomson is an example.

Imagery. Mental pictures produced in the imagination in response to certain words and phrases.

Interior monologue. The expression of a person's thoughts as revealed by a speaker. This may be achieved by adopting the persona of a literary figure, such as the speaker in "Farewell to Barn and Stack and Tree," and writing the thoughts that you imagine would be going through the mind of the speaker.

Ironic understatement. Purposely presenting something less strongly than the facts would warrant, so a situation becomes more obviously ironic.

Irony. Using words in a way that makes them convey the opposite of their usual meaning is *verbal irony*. It would be shown by asking a glum friend, "What puts you in such a sunny mood today?"

In *situation irony*, the result turns out to be the opposite of what you would expect, as when a sharpshooter tries to show off his fancy gun handling and shoots himself in the foot.

Literal. To be taken at its face value; meant to mean exactly what it says.

Literary ballad. Poems modeled after folk ballads but composed by known authors. "O What Is That Sound?" is a literary ballad.

Lyric. Originally, a poem meant to be sung; now, any short, non-narrative poem that expresses emotion. "Those Winter Sundays" by Robert Hayden and "The Best" by Elizabeth Barrett Browning are examples.

Metaphor. A comparison of one thing to another of a different class for the purpose of putting the first in sharper focus through recognition of similarities. "Truth is a phantom" is an example.

Meter. The pattern of stressed and unstressed syllables that is the basis of poetic rhythm. Meter is described in terms of poetic feet in a line.

Iambic monometer (one iambic foot per line)

It's time
To rhyme.

Iambic dimeter (two iambic feet per line)

A sun | ny day
The month | of May,
That's na | ture's way.

Iambic trimeter (three iambic feet per line)

The fu | ture will | not wait.

Iambic tetrameter (four iambic feet per line)

The rich | man has | his mo | tor car,
His coun | try and | his town | estate.

Iambic pentameter (five iambic feet per line)

For thy | sweet love | remem | bered, such | wealth brings
That then | I scorn | to change | my state | with kings.

Note that most poetic feet are made up of one stressed syllable and one or more unstressed syllables. (An exception is the spondee, which has two stressed syllables.) Vertical lines are used to mark off feet. In addition to the iamb (ᵕ ́) used in the examples, other kinds of poetic feet include the anapest (ᵕᵕ ́); the trochee (́ᵕ); and the dactyl (́ᵕᵕ).

Monologue. A prolonged speech by a single person. "The Naming of Cats" is a monologue.

Narrative. The kind of writing that tells a story. Folk ballads like "Johnie Armstrong," literary ballads like "O What Is That Sound?" and poems like "The Sycophantic Fox and Gullible Raven" are narratives.

Negative words. Words used to cause an unfavorable response because of their connotations. Calling someone *pushy* instead of *friendly* shows a negative attitude by a choice made between two words with similar meaning.

Nuance. A shade of meaning that's distinctive to a word. *Colossal, gargantuan,* and *titanic* are adjectives descriptive of something huge, yet all contain different nuances of sense.

Parallel construction. The use of equivalent grammatical expressions to emphasize elements that are parallel in thought. By using sentence patterns that are alike—words parallel with words, phrases with phrases, and clauses with clauses, the poet focuses extra attention on certain key ideas. Lines in Emily Dickinson's "I never saw a moor" illustrate parallel construction.

Paraphrase. A reworded version that runs parallel to the original poem or statement. For example, the first two lines of "On Change of Weathers" are

> And were it for thy profit, to obtain
> All sunshine? No vicissitude of rain?

A paraphrase reads:

> And would it be to your advantage to have
> Nothing but sunshine? No variety with times of rain?

Persona. A term applied to the first-person speaker in a poem or work of fiction. The word *persona* is used to distinguish between the writer and the character who is speaking.

Personification. Giving human qualities and abilities to non-human things, like the sun and nature. "The Tables Turned" by William Wordsworth illustrates this technique.

Poetic foot. A unit in a repeated pattern of stressed and unstressed syllables.

Poetic justice. An unexpected outcome that seems like an ironic trick of fate. In "Ozymandias" by Percy Bysshe Shelley, there is poetic justice in the fact that only a colossal wreck is left, in spite of the boast of the "King of Kings."

Point of view. The choice of spokesman through whose eyes a poem or a story is told. Possibilities are *first person,* told by a speaker identifying himself or herself as *I* ("The Unexplorer") and *third person,* told by an outside narrator ("A La Carte").

Positive words. Words chosen to create a favorable attitude toward a subject. For example, the choices of *inquiring* instead of *nosy,* and *casual* instead of *sloppy* reflect a positive attitude.

Prose. Written or spoken language not having the form or metrical pattern of poetry.

Pun. The humorous use of a word to suggest multiple meanings.

Quatrain. A complete poem or a stanza of four lines. "The First Snow-Fall" by James Russell Lowell is written in quatrains.

> The snow had begun in the gloaming,
> And busily all the night
> Had been heaping field and highway
> With a silence deep and white.

Refining. Polishing or pruning what you write to eliminate unnecessary words that distract from your idea.
Unrefined: The game was for the championship, and our team won it with a basket at the last minute. It was exciting.
Refined: Our team won the championship game with an exciting last-minute basket.

Rhyme. Matching words that have the same or similar end-sounds. For example, *spring* and *wing, hour* and *flower.*

Rhyme scheme. The plan that a poet follows in the choice of rhymes. It is usually identified with letters, a different one being used each time a new rhyme is introduced.

> Once in a golden hour   a
> 　I cast to earth a seed.   b
> Up there came a flower,   a
> 　The people said, a weed.   b
>
> To and fro they went   c
> 　Thro' my garden-bower,   a
> And muttering discontent   c
> 　Cursed me and my flower.   a

Rhythm. The use of a musical beat, involving the alternation of stressed and unstressed syllables, to set the tempo of a poem.

Sarcasm. Harsh or bitter mockery; a purposely cutting remark. You can use sarcasm directly by saying "You're so dumb" or indirectly by "You're so clever," but only the second statement also contains irony.

Satire. Writing that makes fun of a serious situation, such as "Ozymandias" by Percy Bysshe Shelley and "Suicide" by Alice Walker.

Scansion. The act of identifying and marking stressed and unstressed syllables in lines of poetry in order to determine meter. The following illustrates how lines of verse are scanned:

Now tell | us all | about | the war,
And what | they fought | each oth|er for.

Setting. The place and time in which a narrative occurs.

Shakespearean sonnet, also called the *English sonnet*. Its fourteen lines consist of three quatrains, each with its own rhyme scheme, finishing with a rhymed couplet that sums up what has gone before. Its meter is iambic pentameter.

Simile. A type of metaphor that makes an indirect comparison, introduced by *like* or *as*. In "Pretty Words," Elinor Wylie uses a simile when she writes of "honeyed words like bees/ Gilded and sticky, with a little sting."

Sonnet. A poem of fourteen lines written in iambic pentameter (five iambic feet per line) and having one of several traditional rhyme schemes. Sonnets by William Shakespeare and Elizabeth Barrett Browning represent this popular poetic form.

Stanza. A grouping of a certain number of lines, forming a division of a poem. "The Battle of Blenheim" has stanzas of six lines each.

Symbol. Something that stands for something else and, in poetry, enriches meaning. To understand the use of a symbol, you should know what it refers to literally, and then what it stands for. In "The First Snow-Fall" by James Russell Lowell, the snow is real snow but also a symbol of the healing gift of patience that comes to ease the man's sorrow.

Synopsis. A condensed version, a brief summary of a plot, such as might appear in the television listings of a newspaper.

Theme. The subject that a poet "plays upon" to express a poem's underlying idea. Themes may be openly stated or indirect, approached seriously or humorously, and concern matters either trivial or important.

Tone. The attitude a writer expresses toward a subject. Tone may be serious or humorous, tragic or comic. For example, "Dirge" by Percy Bysshe Shelley has a serious tone, while "A Sea Dirge" by Lewis Carroll has a humorous one.

Universality. The quality of appealing to people everywhere, past and present, as a result of expressing common interests, feelings, and concerns.

Index of Titles
and Authors

NTC LANGUAGE ARTS BOOKS

Business Communication
Business Communication Today! *Thomas & Fryar*
Handbook for Business Writing, *Baugh, Fryar, & Thomas*
Meetings: Rules & Procedures, *Pohl*

Dictionaries
British/American Language Dictionary, *Moss*
NTC's Classical Dictionary, *Room*
NTC's Dictionary of Changes in Meaning, *Room*
NTC's Dictionary of Literary Terms, *Morner & Rausch*
NTC's Dictionary of Word Origins, *Room*
NTC's Spell It Right Dictionary, *Downing*
Robin Hyman's Dictionary of Quotations

Essential Skills
Building Real Life English Skills, *Starkey & Penn*
English 93, *Reynolds, Steet, & Guillory*
English Survival Series, *Maggs*
Essential Life Skills, *Starkey & Penn*
Essentials of English Grammar, *Baugh*
Essentials of Reading and Writing English Series
Grammar for Use, *Hall*
Grammar Step-by-Step, *Pratt*
Guide to Better English Spelling, *Furness*
How to be a Rapid Reader, *Redway*
How to Improve Your Study Skills, *Coman & Heavers*
NTC Skill Builders
Reading by Doing, *Simmons & Palmer*
Developing Critical Thinking Skills, *Boostrom*
303 Dumb Spelling Mistakes, *Downing*
TIME: We the People, *ed. Schinke-Llano*
Vocabulary by Doing, *Beckert*

Genre Literature
The Detective Story, *Schwartz*
The Short Story & You, *Simmons & Stern*
Sports in Literature, *Emra*
You and Science Fiction, *Hollister*

Journalism
Getting Started in Journalism, *Harkrider*
Journalism Today! *Ferguson & Patten*

Language, Literature, and Composition
An Anthology for Young Writers, *Meredith*
The Art of Composition, *Meredith*
Creative Writing, *Mueller & Reynolds*
Handbook for Practical Letter Writing, *Baugh*
How to Write Term Papers and Reports, *Baugh*
Literature by Doing, *Tchudi & Yesner*
Lively Writing, *Schrank*
Look, Think & Write, *Leavitt & Sohn*
Poetry by Doing, *Osborn*
Publishing the Literary Magazine, *Klaiman*
Write to the Point! *Morgan*
The Writer's Handbook, *Karls & Szymanski*
Writing by Doing, *Sohn & Enger*
Writing in Action, *Meredith*

Media Communication
Getting Started in Mass Media, *Beckert*
Photography in Focus, *Jacobs & Kokrda*
Television Production Today! *Kirkham*
Understanding Mass Media, *Schrank*
Understanding the Film, *Bone & Johnson*

Mythology
Mythology and You, *Rosenberg & Baker*
Welcome to Ancient Greece, *Millard*
Welcome to Ancient Rome, *Millard*
World Mythology, *Rosenberg*

Speech
Activities for Effective Communication, *LiSacchi*
The Basics of Speech, *Galvin, Cooper, & Gordon*
Contemporary Speech, *HopKins & Whitaker*
Creative Speaking, *Buys et al.*
Creative Speaking Series
Dynamics of Speech, *Myers & Herndon*
Getting Started in Public Speaking, *Prentice & Payne*
Listening by Doing, *Galvin*
Literature Alive! *Gamble & Gamble*
Person to Person, *Galvin & Book*
Public Speaking Today! *Prentice & Payne*
Speaking by Doing, *Buys, Sill, & Beck*

Theatre
Acting & Directing, *Grandstaff*
The Book of Cuttings for Acting & Directing, *Cassady*
The Book of Scenes for Acting Practice, *Cassady*
The Dynamics of Acting, *Snyder & Drumsta*
An Introduction to Modern One-Act Plays, *Cassady*
An Introduction to Theatre and Drama, *Cassady & Cassady*
Play Production Today! *Beck et al.*
Stagecraft, *Beck*

Career Planning
OPPORTUNITIES IN...
Acting Careers
Advertising Careers
Book Publishing Careers
Broadcasting Careers
Business Communications Careers
Film Careers
Journalism Careers
Magazine Publishing Careers
Public Relations Careers
Teaching Careers
Theatrical Design & Production
Writing Careers

How to Write a Winning Résumé
How to Have a Winning Job Interview

For a current catalog and information about our complete line
of language arts books, write:
National Textbook Company
a division of NTC Publishing Group
4255 West Touhy Avenue
Lincolnwood (Chicago), Illinois 60646-1975 U.S.A.